Liv Asplund and Jane Asprusten

KNITTING WITH BEADS
MADE EASY

Simple Techniques, Handy Shortcuts, and
60 Fabulous Projects

TRAFALGAR SQUARE
North Pomfret, Vermont

First published in the United States of America in 2018 by
Trafalgar Square Books
North Pomfret, Vermont 05053

Originally published in Norwegian as *Strikk med perler*.

Copyright © 2016 Cappelen Damm AS
English translation © 2018 Trafalgar Square Books

ISBN: 978-1-57076-849-1

Library of Congress Control Number: 2017960451

Diagrams: Denise Samson
Interior design and layout: Laila Sundet Gundersen
Photography: Guri Pfeifer
Technical editor: May Linn Bang
Translation into English: Carol Huebscher Rhoades

Printed in China

10 9 8 7 6 5 4 3 2 1

CONTENTS

LIFT YOUR SPIRITS WITH ... BEADS?

Have you ever knitted with beads? We hadn't. We can admit it! All the knitting patterns with beads we'd seen began with stringing the beads onto the yarn before you could even cast on the first stitch. They used fine yarn, fine needles, and small glass beads—so easy to miscount, drop, or lose. It just seemed like too much trouble!

We do understand that, now and then, it makes sense to knit with beads the traditional way—all the beads strung on the yarn before you begin. But how much fun is it to knit with yarn that's heavy with beads? Having to slide them down all the time, and watching your beautiful yarn get shredded and rubbed apart by them as you go—not to mention the challenge of stringing the beads on the yarn in the right order (in the opposite order as for the knitting), if there's a bead motif in multiple colors! If even one bead is in the wrong place, the yarn has to be cut and rejoined in the middle of the pattern. So, yes, we'll admit it: We considered knitting with beads time-consuming and tedious work—something we didn't have the patience for.

Except we also have to admit, at the same time, that beads are so lovely! And in the end, we asked ourselves: Must we always stick to fine yarn, fine needles, and tiny beads? Does knitting with beads always have to be done the same way? Couldn't there be a simpler method?

And, of course, there is! We'll show you how you can knit and crochet in beads without first stringing them on the yarn. Just place each bead exactly where you want it to be, in the right color, in the right place; it's easy and straightforward! You can absolutely use light fine yarns and little beads—or chunky textured yarn and big, bright beads. Whatever your heart desires, there's a way to make it work! Knitting with beads can be fast, fun, and simple, and add a little glitz and glamor to any pattern.

Try it, and see if you can't add a little joy to your knitting with beads!

Greetings from Liv and Jane

Basic tips

When beads aren't strung onto the yarn, how do you position them in your knitting? It's actually quite easy: You add the beads to the stitches instead! To slide beads onto stitches, you'll need a crochet hook, dental floss, or a wire needle that looks like a sewing needle—you can make one yourself out of a bit of jewelry wire. You can also use half of a "big eye" beading needle.

KNITTING WITH BEADS & SINGLE-COLOR YARN

Dental Floss

Wire Needles/Big Eye Needles

Crochet Hook

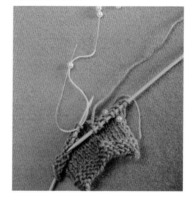

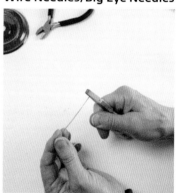

The fastest and easiest way is to use a crochet hook. Place the bead on the hook, slip the stitch from the knitting needle onto the crochet hook, slide the bead down onto the stitch, place the stitch back on the knitting needle, and knit it. For beads with small holes, you'll need a very small hook. We've used needles all the way down to .75 mm, which works well if the yarn isn't too thick.

Dental floss (off-brand from the pharmacy is fine!) works well, too. Place one or more beads onto the floss. Draw the stiff end through the stitch on the knitting needle. Next, insert the floss back into the bead, lift the stitch off the knitting needle, slide the bead down onto the stitch, slip the stitch back onto the needle, remove the floss, and knit the stitch. Make a large knot on the soft end of the dental floss if you've strung a lot of beads onto it.

Make your own wire needles out of jewelry wire. Snip off a piece of wire that's 4¾-6 in / 12-15 cm long, fold it at the center, and you have a beading needle. You can compress the "eye" with pliers if you have them. Insert one leg of the wire needle through the stitch where you want a bead, lift the stitch off the knitting needle, and pop the bead down onto the wire needle and then down onto the stitch. Slip the stitch back onto the needle, remove the wire needle, and knit the stitch.

Big Eye Needles for Beading

A beading needle with a large eye in the center can also be used. Split the needle at the center of the eye and pinch off part of the long ends so you have two usable needles that can work the same way as wire needles, described above. The problem with beading needles is that they're very fine. They work well with fine yarn and beads with small holes, but can quickly become twisted and bent.

Whether the stitch will be purled or knit after the bead has been placed on it varies from pattern to pattern. It usually doesn't matter if the stitch is worked through the back loop (twisted) or front loop (regular knit stitch)—the bead will cover most or all of the stitch.

KNITTING MULTI-COLOR PATTERNS

Beads can also be used in knitting patterns with several colors. They can be placed on stitches using the same methods as for single-color patterns. But it's important to remember that because beads are placed on individual stitches, you must find the right stitches before you can drop beads onto them.

You have your pick of two different methods for placing a bead on the right stitch in a multi-color knitted piece. Either place the bead on the stitch you've just knitted and then continue knitting (see Method 1); or place the bead on the next round when you come to the stitch, which has already been knitted and is just waiting for the bead to be placed on it (see Method 2).

1) Knit the stitch where the bead will be placed, drop the bead onto the stitch, slip the stitch onto the *right* needle and continue knitting without knitting the stitch with the bead (because you have already knitted it).

Maybe it seems like it would be easier to add the bead if you turned the knitted fabric to the wrong side while you're doing it ... Try it and see!

2) Knit the entire round or row where the bead(s) will be placed without adding the bead(s). On the next round/row, when you come to a stitch that will get a bead, drop the bead onto the stitch, place the stitch back on the *left* needle and knit it.

It doesn't matter which method you use! The result will be the same either way: The bead will be in the right place in the pattern. The authors aren't exactly in agreement about which method is best—Jane likes the first method, while Liv prefers the second one. Which one is your favorite?

Shortcuts, tips, and abbreviations

WHAT YOU NEED AND CHARTS

The patterns in this book begin with "Materials"—an overview of the yarn, knitting needles, beads, and anything else you must have to make the project. Because you're knitting with beads, you'll also need a crochet hook, dental floss, or wire/bead needle to place the beads onto the stitches. Additionally, you might want a row counter, paper and a pencil, stitch markers, measuring tape, a little extra yarn for markers, a tapestry needle, and scissors—and possibly more. We haven't listed bead needles and all the other tools in each pattern. We also assume you've knitted before and already know that all charts are read from right to left, and from the bottom up. It's a good idea to read through the whole pattern before you start knitting, to make sure there aren't any unclear details. And we assume that you know how to knit and purl, so we didn't include explanations of how to produce knit and purl stitches.

KNITTING NEEDLES, GAUGE, AND SIZING

If you're going to knit in the round, you need to choose between double-pointed needles, a circular shorter than the knitted piece, or a long circular for magic loop knitting. The patterns in this book that are knitted in the round are worked on double-pointed needled or short circulars.
If you're working back and forth,

you can use straight needles or a circular. We recommend circulars. Straight needles often weigh more, especially if they're long, so the whole knitted garment becomes heavier to work with. Stitches also slide off long and heavy needles more easily. We also like working with wood needles more than metal ones. This is especially important for us when working with the short double-pointed needles we use. No matter what materials your needles are made of, they should have long, pointed tips. You'll soon notice that needles with short, rounded tips are harder to work with when knitting with beads.
In most of the patterns, we only list a stitch count for the gauge. That's because most of the designs (wrist warmers, half gloves, scarves, and loose cowls) fit everyone, no matter the size! You can, of course, change the sizing by using smaller or larger needles. You can also choose a finer or heavier yarn.

YARN

The yarn chosen for most of the designs in this book is from Sandnes Garn (Sandnes). They say that an old love never dies, and we've used Sandnes yarn for as long as we can remember! We knitted our first sweaters with Peer Gynt when we were in grade school. One of us also freelanced as a designer for Sandnes for several years, so we have many ties binding us to the company.

BEADS AND WASHING

The most important consideration for beads you plan to use in knitting is that they have holes big enough for the stitches to pass through, and that they wear well and can be washed. Plastic and glass beads are the most wash- and wear-tolerant. Real pearls (mother-of-pearl) cannot be washed. Wooden beads should be tested with a sample on a knitted swatch.
If you want to machine-wash your beaded knitting, use a nylon net washing bag, low temperature, the wool-wash program on the machine, and wool-safe soap. The only exception is for knitting that will be fulled (see page 110).

FINDING BEADS

The Resources page at the back of the book lists places where you can buy beads. In addition, we've found many beads in our jewelry box, on candle rings, in resale stores, and in chain stores, such as H&M. Such shops often have seasonal sales on jewelry. In general, the jewelry beads you find there are made of plastic and are durable. A long costume jewelry chain will have enough beads for several projects. So, for those of us knitting with beads, the phrase "chain store" has a totally different meaning ...

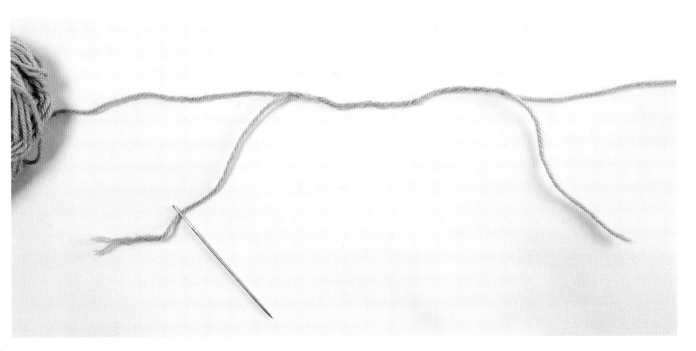

KNITTING TIPS: *Writing a book takes time. Some of the samples in this book were knitted more than a year ago. That means that some of the colors/beads that we used might not be available anymore. These days, though, knitters have so many options to choose from—it's not difficult to find substitutes! Choose your own colors and beads, and create your own unique variations!*

YARN CARE

If the yarn is 100% wool and not superwash treated, you can split about 6 in / 15 cm of the ends on each strand, overlap the strands, lightly dampen them in warm water, and aggressively roll them together between your palms so the fibers will felt together. If the yarn won't felt, you can use a fine tapestry needle to "sew" one end through the other for about 6 in / 15 cm (see photo above). Pull on the yarn to make sure the join is firm.

If you're knitting back and forth, you can avoid splicing the yarn if you start with a new ball of yarn at the beginning of the row. In that case, you can weave in the ends left hanging at the side of the piece afterward.

WEAVING IN YARN ENDS

You can use a tapestry needle to weave in loose yarn ends on the wrong side of the knitted fabric. "Weaving in" is a good description of how the yarn is attached—it is "woven in" on the wrong side.

When knitting with several strands at the same time, the result will be neater and less clumpy if you weave in each individual yarn end separately. If the yarn to be woven in is very thick, you can split it into two lengths so you have two finer ends to weave in instead of one thick one.

ABBREVIATIONS

BO	bind off (= British cast off)
CC	contrast color (pattern color)
ch	chain
cm	centimeter(s)
CO	cast on
dc	double crochet (= British treble crochet)
dpn	double-pointed needles
in	inch(es)
k	knit
k2tog	knit 2 together = right-leaning decrease; 1 st decreased
kf&b	knit into front and then back of same stitch = 1 st increased
m	meter(s)
M1	make 1 = lift strand between 2 sts and knit into back loop
MC	main color (background)
mm	millimeters
p	purl
pm	place marker
psso	pass slipped st over
rem	remain(s)(ing)
rep	repeat(s)
rnd(s)	round(s)
RS	right side
sc	single crochet (= British double crochet)
sl	slip
ssk	(slip 1 knitwise) 2 times, and then knit together through back loops (= slip, slip, knit; left-leaning decrease; 1 st decreased)
st(s)	stitch(es)
tbl	through back loop(s)
tr	treble crochet (= British double treble)
WS	wrong side
wyb	with yarn held in back of work
yo	yarnover

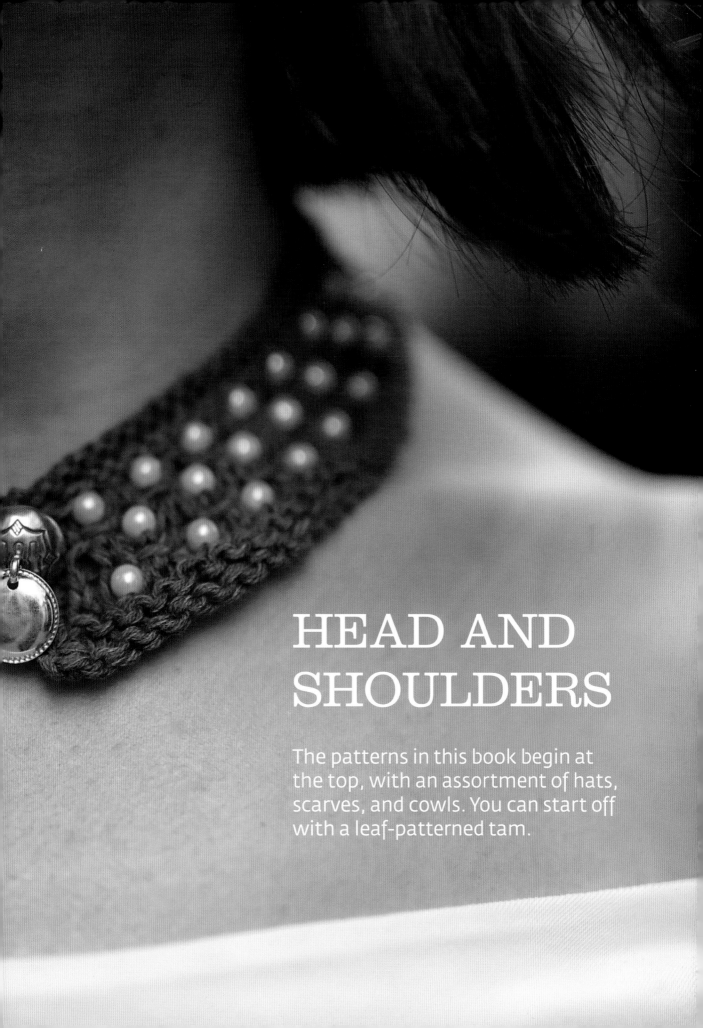

HEAD AND
SHOULDERS

The patterns in this book begin at
the top, with an assortment of hats,
scarves, and cowls. You can start off
with a leaf-patterned tam.

Tam with beaded leaves

What comes first—the beads or the yarn? With this tam, it was the beads. We found earrings on sale at H&M and bought two pairs because the beads were so pretty. They lay in the bead tray until it was time to look for yarn that matched them …

DIFFICULTY LEVEL
Intermediate

FINISHED MEASUREMENTS
Circumference at lower edge: approx. 20 in / 51 cm. Alpaca yarn is very soft and, when knitted, is quite elastic. This sizing will fit most heads. If you want to change the stitch count, you'll need a multiple of 6 sts.

MATERIALS
Yarn:
CYCA #3 (DK, light worsted) Sandnes Garn Alpakka (100% alpaca, 120 yd/110 m / 50 g), Color 5563, 100 g

CYCA #1 (fingering) Sandnes Garn Mini Alpakka (100% alpaca, 164 yd/150 m / 50 g), Color 5244, 50 g

Beads:
51 beads, 5 x 6 mm

NEEDLES
U.S. sizes 4 and 8 / 3.5 and 5 mm: short circulars; size U.S. 8 / 5 mm only: set of 5 dpn

GAUGE
20 sts in stockinette on smaller needles = 4 in / 10 cm.
Adjust needle sizes to obtain correct gauge if necessary.

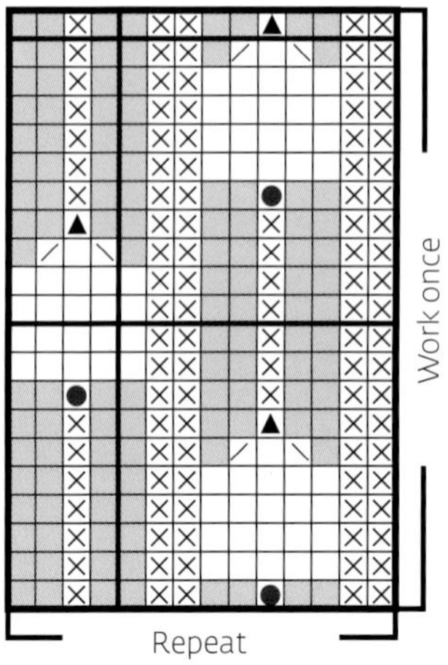

All rounds are shown on the chart

☐ Knit

☒ Purl

◉ Place a bead (see page 6) on the stitch. Work (k1, yo, k1, yo, k1) in the stitch after the bead has been placed on stitch = 5 leaf stitches in the bead stitch.

◺ K2tog tbl

◹ K2tog

▲ Sl 1, k2tog, psso

▨ No stitch

(Chart labels: **Work once** on right side, **Repeat** below chart)

INSTRUCTIONS

This tam is knitted in the round with a stockinette band at the lower edge. The edge, which is knitted with 1 strand of Alpakka, is turned at the foldline, and the facing is sewn down by hand in finishing. The rest of the hat is knitted with two strands of yarn, one strand of each weight.

With smaller circular, CO 102 sts. Join, being careful not to twist cast-on row. Pm for beginning of rnd. Knit around until piece measures approx. 1½ in / 4 cm or the height you want for the band. Purl 1 rnd (= foldline) and continue in stockinette until the piece is the same length on both sides of the foldline. Change to larger circular and two strands of yarn—1 strand each Alpakka and Mini Alpakka. Purl 3 rnds. Now work the leaf motif following the chart. Before beginning the crown shaping, purl 1 rnd, decreasing 2 sts evenly spaced around = 100 sts rem. Change to dpn when sts no longer fit around circular.

Crown Shaping

Decrease Rnd 1: (P2, p2tog) around = 75 sts rem. Purl 4 rnds without deceasing.
Decrease Rnd 2: (P1, p2tog) around = 50 sts rem. Purl 4 rnds without deceasing.
Decrease Rnd 3: (P2tog) around = 25 sts rem. Purl 3 rnds without deceasing.
Decrease Rnd 4: (P2tog) around to last st, p1 = 13 sts rem.
Purl 1 rnd without deceasing.

Finishing

Cut yarn, leaving an 11¾ in / 30 cm end.
Draw the end through rem sts and tighten. Fold the band at the foldline and, by hand, sew down the facing on WS. Weave in all yarn ends. Gently steam press the lower band and the shaped crown. Do not press the leaf patterning.

Easy everyday hat

Knit an easy and fun hat for yourself that you can wear every day. With a few beads on the stitches to add a little flash, you won't want to take it off! The hat has 100 stitches around and 50 rounds after the ribbing—it's a basic pattern that you can use again and again and again ...

DIFFICULTY LEVEL
Easy

FINISHED MEASUREMENTS
Size M: Circumference 20¾ in / 52.5 cm

MATERIALS
Yarn:
CYCA #3 (DK, light worsted) Sandnes Garn Smart (100% wool, 108 yd/99 m / 50 g), Color 6162, 100 g

CYCA #1 (fingering) Sandnes Garn Sisu (80% wool, 20% polyamide, 191 yd/175 m / 50 g), Color 1088, 50 g

Beads:
20 beads, approx. 8 mm

NEEDLES
U.S. sizes 4 and 7 / 3.5 and 4.5 mm: short circulars; size U.S. 7 / 4.5 mm only: set of 5 dpn

GAUGE
19 sts in stockinette on larger needles = 4 in / 10 cm.
Adjust needle sizes to obtain correct gauge if necessary.

INSTRUCTIONS
This hat is worked with two strands of yarn held together, one strand of each weight. The beads for the hat were taken from a long necklace (H&M). The stitches are knitted after the beads have been placed on them. All the decreases are worked with k2tog.

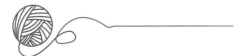

With smaller circular, CO 100 sts. Join, being careful not to twist cast-on row. Pm for beginning of rnd. Knit 4 rnds. Now work 5 rnds in k1tbl, p1 ribbing. Change to larger circular.

Rnds 1-4: Knit.

Rnd 5: Knit, placing 1 bead on every 25th st (see page 6), with the first bead on the 13th stitch.

Rnds 6-9: Knit.

Rnd 10: K24, place bead, k49, place bead; knit to end of rnd.

Rnds 11-14: Knit.

Rnd 15: K49, place bead, k49, place bead.

Rnds 16-19: Knit.

Rnd 20: Work as for Rnd 5.

Rnds 21-24: Knit.

Rnd 25: Work as for Rnd 10.

Rnd 26: Knit around, and, *at the same time*, decrease 5 sts evenly spaced around = 95 sts rem.

NOTE: Change to dpn when sts no longer fit around circular.

Rnds 27-28: Knit.

Rnd 29: Knit around, and, *at the same time*, decrease 5 sts evenly spaced around = 90 sts rem.

Rnd 30: Knit around, and, *at the same time*, place 1 bead directly over the beads on Rnd 15.

Rnd 31: Knit.

Rnd 32: K9 between each decrease, decreasing 8 times total = 82 sts rem.

Rnds 33-34: Knit.

Rnd 35: Knit around, and, *at the same time*, place 1 bead directly over the beads on Rnd 5, *and* decrease 2 sts between each bead = 74 sts rem.

Rnds 36-37: Knit.

Rnd 38: Knit around, and, at the same time, decrease 8 sts evenly spaced around = 66 sts rem.

Rnds 39-49: Knit.

Rnd 50: (K4, k2tog) = 55 sts rem.

Finishing

Cut yarn, leaving an end 11¾ in / 30 cm long. Draw end through rem sts and tighten well. Weave in all ends neatly on WS.

Black hat with felted wool beads

A black hat can actually be very colorful. When you knit in felted wool beads in a variety of colors, you get a fun and unique black hat.

DIFFICULTY LEVEL
Easy

FINISHED MEASUREMENTS
Size S/M: Circumference approx. 21 in / 53 cm

MATERIALS
Yarn:
CYCA #3 (DK, light worsted) Sandnes Garn Alpakka (100% alpaca, 120 yd/110 m / 50 g), Color 1099, 100 g

Beads and Notions:
40 felted wool beads in an assortment of colors, approx. ½ in / 12 mm in diameter (Creativ Company) Awl (see Tips on next page)

NEEDLES
U.S. sizes 2.5 and 4 / 3 and 3.5 mm: 16 in / 40 cm circulars; size U.S. 4 / 3.5 mm only: set of 5 dpn

GAUGE
20 sts in garter st on smaller needles = 4 in / 10 cm.
Adjust needle sizes to obtain correct gauge if necessary.

INSTRUCTIONS
This hat is worked in the round on a short circular needle. When shaping the crown, change to dpn when sts no longer fit around the circular.

With smaller circular, CO 100 sts. Work back and forth in garter stitch (knit all rows) for approx. 1½ in / 4 cm. Change to larger circular. Join, being careful not to twist cast-on row. Pm for beginning of rnd. Knit 4 rnds. Purl 1 rnd. Knit 2 rnds.

BEAD TIPS
The felted wool beads that I used did not have any holes, so I made some by sticking an awl through each bead. Next, I inserted a knitting needle into the hole and widened it to make it easier to drop the bead onto a stitch.

Now knit in the felted wool beads (see page 6). The wool beads are placed as follows:

1st Rnd with beads: *(K9, place 1 bead on the 10th st) around. Knit 3 rnds without beads.

2nd Rnd with beads: K4, place 1 bead on 5th st, (k9, place 1 bead on the 10th st) until 5 sts rem, end k5. Knit 3 rnds without beads*.

Rep from * to * once more, so there are 4 rows of felted wool beads on the hat. Purl 1 rnd. Now knit around until the hat is approx. 7 in / 18 cm long.

Shaping Crown
Decrease Rnd 1: (K8, k2tog) around = 90 sts rem.
Knit 1 rnd.
Decrease Rnd 2: (K7, k2tog) around = 80 sts rem.
Knit 1 rnd.
Continue decreasing on every other rnd, with 1 less st between decreases until 10 sts rem.
Last Decrease Rnd: (K2tog) around.

Finishing
Cut yarn, leaving an end 8 in / 20 cm long. Draw end through rem sts and tighten well. Seam the short ends of the garter band. Weave in all ends neatly on WS.

Hat and wrist warmers with buttons

Perhaps you also have a large or small collection of buttons? Now you can use up some of those buttons by knitting them onto—for example—a hat and a pair of wrist warmers. Use buttons that aren't too heavy! For our set, we used metallic-looking plastic buttons backed with metal loops.

DIFFICULTY LEVEL
Easy

FINISHED MEASUREMENTS
Hat: Size M, circumference approx. 21¾ in / 55 cm
Wrist Warmers: approx. 5½ in / 14 cm long and approx. 7 in / 18 cm in circumference

MATERIALS
Yarn:
CYCA #3 (DK, light worsted) Sandnes Garn Merinoull (100% Merino wool, 114 yd/104 m / 50 g), Color 1099, 100 g

Buttons:
28 buttons, plastic, metallic coating, metal loop backs: 16 buttons for the hat and 12 for the wrist warmers

NEEDLES
U.S. size 4 / 3.5 mm: 16 in / 40 cm circular and set of 5 dpn

GAUGE
19 sts in stockinette = 4 in / 10 cm.
Adjust needle size to obtain correct gauge if necessary.

INSTRUCTIONS

HAT
This hat can easily be enlarged or made smaller with more or fewer stitches. Place the buttons as for beads (see page 6). The hat is worked around in stockinette on a short circular. When shaping the crown, change to dpn when sts no longer fit around the circular.

With circular, CO 100 sts. Join, being careful not to twist cast-on row. Pm for beginning of rnd. Knit around for 2½-2¾ in / 6-7 cm.
Continue working around in stockinette, and, *at the same time*, place the buttons as follows: (K5, place 1 button on the 6th st) around = 16 buttons. There will be 9 sts between the first and last buttons.
After the button rnd, continue working around in stockinette until hat is approx. 8 in / 20 cm long.

Shaping Crown
Decrease Rnd 1: (K8, k2tog) around = 90 sts rem. Knit 1 rnd.
Decrease Rnd 2: (K7, k2tog) around = 80 sts rem. Knit 1 rnd.
Continue decreasing on every other rnd, with 1 less st between decreases until 10 sts rem.
Last Decrease Rnd: (K2tog) around.

Finishing
Cut yarn, leaving an end 8 in / 20 cm long. Draw end through rem sts and tighten well.
Weave in all ends neatly on WS.

WRIST WARMERS
The wrist warmers are worked around in stockinette with yarn left over from the hat.
Make both alike.

With dpn, CO 40 sts. Divide sts onto dpn and join, being careful not to twist cast-on row. Pm for beginning of rnd. Work around in stockinette until piece is approx. 1½ in / 4 cm long. Place buttons as follows: (K5, place button on the 6th st) around = 6 buttons. There will be 9 sts between the first and last buttons. Continue around in stockinette until wrist warmer is approx. 5½ in / 14 cm long or to desired length. BO loosely.

Finishing:
Cut yarn, leaving an end 8 in / 20 cm long. Weave in all ends neatly on WS.

Light gray set with hat and wrist warmers

This light gray set will complement most other colors and so is supremely wearable.

DIFFICULTY LEVEL
Intermediate

FINISHED MEASUREMENTS
Hat: Size M, circumference approx. 21¾ in / 55 cm. If you want a larger or smaller hat, add or subtract stitches. The stitch count should be a multiple of 4 sts.

Wrist Warmers: approx. 6 in / 15 cm long and approx. 7 in / 18 cm in circumference

MATERIALS
Yarn:
CYCA #3 (DK, light worsted) Garn Studio (Drops) Karisma (100% wool, 109 yd/100 m / 50 g), color 8267, 100 g

Beads:
160 plastic beads (mother-of-pearl), approx. 5 mm: 96 beads for the hat and 64 beads for the wrist warmers (Creativ Company)

NEEDLES
U.S. size 6 / 4 mm: 16 in / 40 cm circular and set of 5 dpn

GAUGE
18 sts in stockinette = 4 in / 10 cm.
Adjust needle size to obtain correct gauge if necessary.

INSTRUCTIONS

HAT
The hat is worked in the round on a short circular. Change to dpn when sts no longer fit around circular.

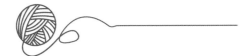

With circular, CO 96 sts. Join, being careful not to twist cast-on row. Pm for beginning of rnd. Knit around in stockinette for approx. 2 in / 5 cm.

Continue working around in charted pattern and then work for approx. 3½ in / 9 cm in stockinette. The entire hat will be about 8 in / 20 cm high.

Shaping Crown:
Decrease Rnd 1: (K10, k2tog) around = 88 sts rem.
Knit 1 rnd.
Decrease Rnd 2: (K9, k2tog) around = 80 sts rem.
Knit 1 rnd.
Continue decreasing on every other rnd, with 1 less st between decreases until 16 sts rem.

Finishing
Cut yarn, leaving an end 9¾ in / 25 cm long. Draw end through rem sts and tighten well. Weave in all ends neatly on WS.

WRIST WARMERS
The wrist warmers are worked around in stockinette with sts divided onto four dpn. Make both alike.

With dpn, CO 32 sts. Divide sts onto dpn and join, being careful not to twist cast-on row. Pm for beginning of rnd. Work around in stockinette until piece is approx. 1½ in / 4 cm long. Work the charted pattern and then continue in stockinette for approx. 2¼ in / 5.5 cm or to desired length. BO loosely.

Finishing:
Cut yarn, leaving an end 8 in / 20 cm long. Weave in all ends neatly on WS.

☐   Knit

☒   Purl

◯   Yarnover

◉   Bead (see page 6). Knit the st after the bead has been placed

⧄   K2tog

Repeat

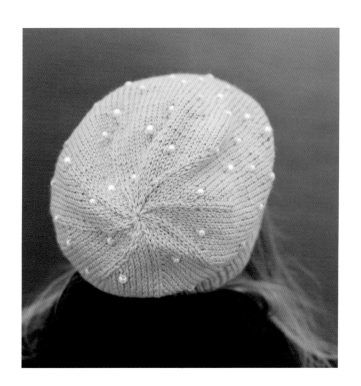

Light blue slouchy hat and wrist warmers

This hat has seed stitch ribbing that's tighter than regular ribbing, which means it'll be good at keeping your ears warm!

DIFFICULTY LEVEL
Intermediate

FINISHED MEASUREMENTS
Hat: Size S, circumference approx. 20½ in / 52 cm.
Wrist Warmers: approx. 4¼ in / 11 cm long and approx. 6¾ in / 17 cm in circumference

MATERIALS
Yarn:
CYCA #3 (DK, light worsted) Sandnes Garn Smart (100% wool, 108 yd/99 m / 50 g), Color 5904, 100 g

Beads:
160-170 plastic beads (mother-of-pearl), 5-8 mm (Creativ Company): 90-100 beads, 5-8 mm for

the hat and 64 beads, approx. 5 mm, for the wrist warmers

NEEDLES
U.S. sizes 4 and 6 / 3.5 and 4 mm: 16 in / 40 cm circulars; U.S. size 6 / 4 mm only: set of 5 dpn

GAUGE
16 sts in seed st ribbing on smaller needles = 4 in / 10 cm.
Adjust needle sizes to obtain correct gauge if necessary.

INSTRUCTIONS

HAT
The hat is worked in the round on a short circular. Change to dpn when sts no longer fit around circular.

With smaller circular, CO 84 sts. Join, being careful not to twist cast-on row. Pm for beginning of rnd. Knit around in seed stitch ribbing as follows:

Rnd 1: (K4, p1, k1, p1) around.
Rnd 2: (K4, k1, p1, k1) around

Rep these 2 rnds until the ribbing measures 4-4¾ in / 10-12 cm.
Change to larger circular. Knit 1 rnd, increasing 24 sts evenly spaced around = 108 sts.
Continue working around in stockinette, and, *at the same time*, add the beads randomly (see page 6). When hat is approx. 8 in / 20 cm high, begin shaping crown.

Shaping Crown:
Decrease Rnd 1: (K10, k2tog) around = 99 sts rem.
Knit 1 rnd.
Decrease Rnd 2: (K9, k2tog) around = 90 sts rem.
Knit 1 rnd.
Decrease Rnd 3: (K8, k2tog) around = 81 sts rem.
Knit 1 rnd.
Continue decreasing on every other rnd, with 1 less st between decreases until 18 sts rem.
Last Decrease Rnd: (K2tog) around.

Finishing
Cut yarn, leaving an end 8 in / 20 cm long. Draw end through rem sts and tighten well.
Weave in all ends neatly on WS.

WRIST WARMERS
The wrist warmers are worked around in stockinette with sts divided onto four dpn.
Make both alike.

With larger dpn, CO 28 sts. Divide sts onto dpn and join, being careful not to twist cast-on row. Pm for beginning of rnd. Work 2 rnds in seed stitch ribbing as for hat. On the 3rd rnd, place a bead on each of the center knit sts in the seed st column (4 beads per rnd). Knit the st after the bead has been placed. Work 3 rnds without beads. On the 4th rnd, place beads as for Rnd 3. Continue with beads on every 4th rnd until the wrist warmer is approx. 4¼ in / 11 cm long or desired length. Work 3 rnds without beads. BO loosely.

Finishing:
Cut yarn, leaving an end 8 in / 20 cm long. Draw end through last st and weave in all ends neatly on WS.

Hat and mitts set with beads all lined up

Heavy yarn and big needles combined with a simple structure in knit and purl stitches—you'll have this set knit up in no time!

DIFFICULTY LEVEL
Intermediate

FINISHED MEASUREMENTS
Hat: Circumference approx. 19 in / 48 cm and height approx. 9¾ in / 25 cm. The structure is very elastic, so this size will fit most heads.
Mitts: before seaming, approx. 7¼ x 7¼ in / 18.5 x 18.5 cm

MATERIALS
Yarn:
CYCA #5 (Bulky) Sandnes Garn Alfa (85% wool, 15% mohair, 65 yd/59 m / 50 g), Color 1053, 100 g *each* for the hat and wrist warmers = 200 g total

Beads:
84-90 Kongomix beads, 10 mm (Creativ Company): 54-60 beads for the hat and 30 beads for the wrist warmers

NEEDLES
U.S. size 13 / 9 mm for the hat and U.S. size 11 / 7 mm for the wrist warmers: straight or circular needles

GAUGE
Hat: 15 sts pattern on U.S. 13 / 9 mm needles = 4 in / 10 cm.
Mitts: 17 sts on U.S. 11 / 7 mm needles = 4 in / 10 cm.
Adjust needle sizes to obtain correct gauge if necessary.

INSTRUCTIONS
STRUCTURE PATTERN
Slip the first st of every row for an edge st. Work the sts between the edge sts as follows:

Row 1 (RS): Knit and place beads on this row (see page 6). Knit the st after placing the bead.

Row 2 (WS): (K2tog) across until 1 st rem, knit last st (edge st).

Row 3: (K1, p1) in each st until 1 st rem, knit last st (edge st).

Row 4: Purl across.

Rep these 4 rows (= 1 rep).

HAT
The hat is worked back and forth and later seamed up the center back.

With U.S. size 13 / 9 mm needles, CO 40 sts (= the height of the hat) and knit 2 rows for the seam allowance. The rest of the hat is worked in the Structure Pattern above and the beads are placed on Row 1 of the pattern on *every other rep of Row 1*. The outermost 7 sts (6 sts + the edge st) at each side do not have beads. *Place 1 bead on the next st, k4*. Rep from * to * until you've placed 6 beads on the row, knit to end of row. Continue in pattern as est. After 8 rows of beads, try the hat on to see if you need to knit more rows. On the sample in the photos, there are 9 rows of beads. When ready to finish, knit 1 row as a seam allowance and BO, matching tension to cast-on row so the bind-off and cast-on will be the same length. Seam the hat up the center back by hand, with RS facing RS, using small sts and a narrow seam. Weave in all yarn ends neatly on WS. With doubled yarn, sew a basting st along the edge that will be the top of the hat. Baste through the sts inside the edge sts on the WS. Draw the hat together at the top and knot the ends of the basting yarn on the inside of the hat.

MITTS WITH BEADS ON THE BACK OF THE HAND
The mitts are worked as for the hat but with smaller needles. Even if you have yarn leftover from the hat, you should make these with a new ball of yarn.

Right Mitt
With U.S. size 11 / 7 mm needles, CO 32 sts (the length of the mitt) and work 2 repeats of the structure pattern without beads. Work 3 pattern repeats with beads on Row 1 of each rep. Place the first bead on 7th st (including edge st) and then k4 between beads until there 5 beads total on the row. Knit to end of row.

Work 4 repeats without beads. BO on the next RS row. The purl row before the bind-off helps ensure that the bind-off and cast-on edges will be the same length.

Left Mitt
Work as for right mitt but begin with 5 pattern repeats without beads and then work 3 repeats with beads. Work 1 rep without beads and BO.

Finishing
Seam the mitts by hand with RS facing out and edges abutted. Begin at the finger opening and sew down 1½ in / 4 cm; leave a 2 in / 5 cm space open for the thumb and then seam to the end of the cuff. Weave in all ends neatly on WS.

*The mitts feature three rows of
beads on the back of the hand.*

Black ear warmer with transparent beads

Here's the solution for when you go out on a cold winter evening and don't want to spoil your chic look with a close-fitting hat.

DIFFICULTY LEVEL
Intermediate

FINISHED MEASUREMENTS
Approx. 4¼ in / 11 cm wide and approx. 16½ in / 42 cm in circumference

MATERIALS
Yarn:
CYCA #3 (DK, light worsted) Sandnes Garn Al-pakka (100% alpaca, 120 yd/110 m / 50 g), Color 1099, 50 g

Beads:
75 transparent faceted beads, about 8 mm (these came from a candle ring)

NEEDLES
U.S. size 4 / 3.5 mm: short circular

GAUGE
The gauge is not important for this ear warmer. The knitting technique produces a very elastic fabric, so the ear warmer should be slightly tight when you try it on before you bind off.

INSTRUCTIONS

Read through the entire pattern before you begin knitting. The ear warmer is worked back and forth sideways and then seamed. Bead placement: Beads are placed on the 6th pattern row, on the 3rd, 15th, and 27th sts (see page 6). Drop the bead onto the stitch first and then knit the st through back loop = twisted knit.

CO 29 sts.
Row 1: K2, purl to last 2 sts, end k2.
Row 2: K2, M1 between the 2nd and 3rd sts, k4, k2tog, k2tog tbl, k4, M1, k1, M1, k4, k2tog, k2tog tbl, k4, M1, k2.
Row 3: Knit across.
Row 4: Work as for Row 1.
Row 5: Work as for Row 2.
Row 6: Work as for Row 3.
Rep Rows 1-6, placing beads on every 6th row as described above. Continue in pattern until ear warmer fits around head. BO loosely. Cut yarn, leaving an end approx. 8 in / 20 cm long. Draw end through last st. Seam down center back. Weave in all yarn ends neatly on WS.

With one ball of Sisu

Easy, garter stitch, single-color and comfy scarves with pointed tips—and beads! One ball of yarn, a pattern, a long circular, an evening's work, and a bowl of beads is all you need. How many can you make?

DIFFICULTY LEVEL
Intermediate

FINISHED MEASUREMENTS
The scarves measure approx. 17¾ x 43¼ in / 45 x 110 cm. The diagonal side edges are approx. 27½ in / 70 cm long.

MATERIALS
Yarn:
CYCA #1 (fingering), Sandnes Garn Sisu (80% wool, 20% polyamide, 191 yd/175 m / 50 g), 50 g for 1 scarf

White scarf: Color 1001, beads, 8 mm (Søstrene Grene)
Blue scarf: Color 6324, beads, 8 mm (Søstrene Grene)

Black scarf: Color 1099, beads from a pack of bead mix (Perlemix), 7-11 mm (Creativ Company)
Yellow scarf: Color 2015, star-shaped beads (TGR)

Beads:
Approx. 70 beads—see Bead Tips on page 37

NEEDLES
U.S. size 13 / 9 mm: long circular

GAUGE
10 garter ridges on U.S. size 13 / 9 mm needle = approx. 4 in / 10 cm.
Adjust needle size to obtain correct gauge if necessary.

INSTRUCTIONS
The scarves are knitted back and forth in garter stitch on a long circular needle. Place the beads

These scarves are knitted
with fine yarn on small
needles. One 50-gram
ball is enough for one!
These knitted pieces grow
quickly. Wear the scarves
one at a time or wrap
and tie them together for
extra warmth and stylish
neckwear.

(see page 6) randomly all over, with most on the points
and along the diagonal edges.
Knit the stitch after it has a bead placed on it.

CO 3 sts and knit back. All rem rows are worked as:
Sl 1, knit until 2 sts rem, kf&b k1.
Rep this row until almost all the yarn has been used. One general rule suggests that you need 4 times the width of the knitted
piece to work the next row. However, so the edge here doesn't
draw in, you have to bind off rather loosely. That means that
you should start binding off when the remaining yarn is at least
6 times the width. For the samples here, the binding off began
when there were 96-98 stitches. Finish by weaving in all yarn
ends neatly on the WS.

With two balls of Alfa

Tube scarf, ring scarf, circle scarf—beloved children have many names, and, in this case, come in all sizes and colors! This scarf is great for wearing when it's cold and gray. It'll perk up your whole outfit. It's no wonder that scarves like this are so popular! Quick and easy, with two balls of Alfa yarn.

DIFFICULTY LEVEL
Intermediate

FINISHED MEASUREMENTS
The scarf is approx. 6¼ in / 16 cm wide, with a circumference of approx. 47¼ in / 120 cm.

MATERIALS
Yarn:
CYCA #5 (Bulky) Sandnes Garn Alfa (85% wool, 15% mohair, 65 yd/59 m / 50 g), Color 4063, 100 g

Beads:
Approx. 55 beads (see Bead Tips on page 41).

NEEDLES
U.S. size 15 / 10 mm: straight needles

GAUGE
10 sts in seed st on U.S. 15 / 10 mm needles = 4 in / 10 cm.
Adjust needle size to obtain correct gauge if necessary.

INSTRUCTIONS
The scarf is worked back and forth in seed stitch; the short ends are seamed by hand afterwards.

CO 17 sts. All the rows are worked the same way: Always slip the first st on every row as an edge st. Inside the edge sts, work (k1, p1) until 1 st rem; always end with p1.
Work 3-4 rows before placing the first beads

(see page 6). Place the beads as you see fit, but to make sure all the beads show well, mark one side of the scarf as the right side. Place a bead after a purl st on the RS and then knit the st after the bead has been placed. That means that any beads you place on the WS must be placed after a knit st, and the st purled after the bead is placed. Continue as est until rem yarn is about 5 times the width of the fabric. BO. By hand, seam the two short ends with edges abutted. Weave in all ends neatly on WS.

BEAD TIPS

This heavy Alfa yarn needs beads with large holes. For this sample, we used a bead mix (Perlemix from Creativ Company). The flattest beads were used both singly and in pairs on the same stitch.

Zippered cowl

If you insert a separating zipper at the neck, you won't need to pull the cowl over your head when taking it on and off!

DIFFICULTY LEVEL
Advanced

FINISHED MEASUREMENTS
The cowl is approx. 21¾ x 9 in / 55 x 23 cm

MATERIALS
Yarn:
CYCA #5 (Bulky) Sandnes Garn Alfa (85% wool, 15% mohair, 65 yd/59 m / 50 g), Color 1088, 100 g

Beads:
Red and metallic dyed beads (see Bead Tips on page 43)

Notions:
Separating zipper, 8 in / 20 cm long; black sewing thread (or color to match cowl) and sewing needle.

NEEDLES
U.S. size 11 / 7 mm: circular or straight needles

GAUGE
13 sts in seed st on U.S. 11 / 7 mm needles = 4 in / 10 cm.

Adjust needle size to obtain correct gauge if necessary.

INSTRUCTIONS
The cowl is worked back and forth in seed stitch. We recommend a circular rather than long straight needles.

CO 71 sts. All rows are worked the same way: Always slip the first st as an edge st. Inside the edge sts, work (k1, p1) until 1 st rem; always end with p1.
Work for approx. 1 in / 2.5 cm without beads (see page 6). Place the beads as you see fit, but to make sure all the beads show well, mark one side of the scarf as the right side. Place a bead after a purl st on the RS and then knit the st after the bead has been placed. That means that any beads you place on the WS must be placed after a knit st, and the st purled after the bead is placed. Continue as est until piece is approx. 8 in / 20.5 cm long. Continue to total height (9 in / 23 cm) without beads. BO on WS.
BO. Weave in all ends neatly on WS. Sew in the zipper by hand with black sewing thread.

Wear the cowl with the zipper closed, fold it down with the zipper half open, or wear the cowl with the opening at the bottom.

BEAD TIPS
For this model, we used 37 metallic-dyed beads from a pack of bead mix (Perlemix, Creativ Company), plus 11 red wood beads, 8 mm.

Easy lace scarf

An airy shawl/scarf. It'll be just as lovely to have around your neck on a cold winter day as over your shoulders on a chilly September evening.

DIFFICULTY LEVEL
Intermediate

FINISHED MEASUREMENTS
This scarf is approx. 17¾ in / 45 cm wide and approx. 59 in / 150 cm long.

MATERIALS
Yarn:
CYCA #1 (fingering) Sandnes Garn Mini Alpakka (100% alpaca, 164 yd/150 m / 50 g), Color 1001, 150 g

Beads:
100-120 beads, approx. 5-8 mm (those shown came from a necklace)

NEEDLES
U.S. size 10 / 6 mm: circular

GAUGE
Gauge is not important for this project.

INSTRUCTIONS
Read through the instructions all the way to the end before you begin to knit. The shawl/scarf is worked back and forth on a circular needle. The beads are placed randomly on the second row of garter stitch in the pattern. For more on bead placement, see page 6.

CO 50 sts. Begin with the lace pattern.
Rows 1-2: Knit.
Row 3: K2 (edge sts), yo, sl 1, k1, psso. Rep from * to * until 2 sts rem and end k2 (edge sts).
Row 4: Work as for Row 3.
Repeat these 4 rows (= 1 rep) with beads placed on the 2nd row in pattern. After placing a bead, knit the st. Work as est until scarf measures approx. 59 in / 150 cm long or to desired length. BO loosely. Cut yarn, leaving an end 8 in / 20 cm long; draw end through last st. Weave in all ends neatly on WS.

Loop stitch fur collar

Have you made "fur" with loop stitches before? If so, you know it's easy! If you've never tried it, here's your chance. This collar is worked back and forth on short needles and buttoned at center front.

DIFFICULTY LEVEL
Advanced

FINISHED MEASUREMENTS
Brown collar: approx. 3½ x 19 in / 9 x 48 cm. Each loop is about 1 in / 2.5 cm high
Black collar: approx. 4 x 26¾ in / 10 x 68 cm. Each loop is about 1 in / 2.5 cm high

MATERIALS
Yarn:
Brown collar: CYCA #5 (bulky) Sandnes Garn Tweed (40% alpaca, 32% Viscose, 20% Polyamide, 8% wool, 164 yd/150 m / 50 g), Color 3090, 50 g
Black collar:
CYCA #5 (bulky) Sandnes Garn Tweed (40% alpaca, 32% Viscose, 20% Polyamide, 8% wool, 164 yd/150 m / 50 g), Color 1100, 50 g
+

CYCA #2 (fingering) Sandnes Garn Tynn merinoull (Fine Merino wool) (100% Merino wool, 191 yd/175 m / 50 g), Color 1099, 50 g

Beads:
Brown collar: 26 beads, 10 mm (Creativ Company) + 3 shank buttons (approx. 5/8 in / 15 mm) in same color as yarn
Black collar: 34 wood beads, 12 mm (Creativ Company) + 1 black shank button, approx. ¾ in / 17 mm

NEEDLES
Brown collar: U.S. size 10 / 6 mm: short straight needles
Black collar: U.S. size 11 / 7 mm: short straight needles

Knitted loops turn
towards the wrong
side of the fabric.
That makes the collar
look especially full.

GAUGE

Brown collar: 9 sts in loop knitting on U.S. size 10 / 6 mm needles = 3¼ in / 8 cm.
Black collar: 9 sts in loop knitting on U.S. size 11 / 7 mm needles = 3¾ in / 9.5 cm.
Adjust needle size to obtain correct gauge if necessary.

INSTRUCTIONS

Loop Knitting
Row 1 (RS): Sl 1 (edge st), k1, k1 but do not slip st off left needle, bring yarn between the needles and make a loop approx. 1 in / 2.5 cm high, from left to right, and sl yarn back again. Hold the loop in place with your left thumb or hold the yarn loop around your thumb. K1 tbl in the same st as before. Slip the st off the needle and the loop off your thumb. Slip the two nearest sts (that you have just knit) from the right needle to the left needle and k2tog tbl. Rep from * to * until 2 sts rem, end row with k2.
Row 2 (WS): Sl 1 (edge st), purl to end of row.
Rep these 2 rows for pattern.

BROWN COLLAR
The collar is worked with 2 strands of yarn held together. Take 1 strand from the inside of the ball and the other from the outside of the ball. The beads are placed on the WS (see page 6) on every 4th row = every other row of purl sts. Purl the st after placing bead.

CO 11 sts (9 sts + 1 edge st at each side). Knit 2 rows. Now continue in loop knitting.
1st bead row: Place 1 bead on the 4th st (including edge st) and on 8th st.
2nd bead row: Place 1 bead on 6th st (including edge st).

Continue as est until collar is approx. 18½ in / 47 cm long and there are 2 rows of loops after the last bead row. After the last purl row, knit 1 row and then BO. On this short end, the knitting is open enough between the loops that you don't need buttonholes. Sew the buttons evenly spaced to the opposite short end. Weave in all yarn ends neatly on WS.

BLACK COLLAR
This collar is worked as for the brown one but with larger needles and 3 strands of yarn (2 strands of Tweed and 1 strand of Tynn Merinoull) held together. Instead of three buttons, one shank button is sewn securely at the top of the side where the knitting began.
The beads for this collar are placed on the center st of the row, on the first and last bead rows. Otherwise, follow the instructions for the brown collar and work until the collar measures approx. 26½ in / 67 cm or until yarn is almost used up. On our model, we bound off on the row after the last purl row and there was exactly enough Tweed to weave in the ends.

Long star-stitch scarf

This warm scarf is knitted on big needles with two strands of yarn held together. Even though it's long, it's a quick knit. And who says scarves need to be the same at both ends?

DIFFICULTY LEVEL
Advanced

FINISHED MEASUREMENTS
The scarf measures approx. 7¾ x 78 in / 19.5 x 200 cm

MATERIALS
Yarn:
CYCA #5 (bulky) Sandnes Garn Fritidsgarn (100% wool, 77 yd/70 m / 50 g), 100 g *each* colors 1099 and 6071
+
CYCA #1 (fingering) Sandnes Garn Mini Alpakka (100% alpaca, 164 yd/150 m / 50 g), 50 g *each* colors 1099 and 6071

Beads:
76 black wood beads, 12 mm (Creativ Company)

NEEDLES
U.S. size 15 / 10 mm: circular + 2 dpn

GAUGE
14 star stitches with 1 strand of each yarn held together on U.S. size 15 / 10 mm needles = approx. 4 in / 10 cm. Adjust needles size to obtain correct gauge if necessary.

INSTRUCTIONS

Star Pattern
Sl 1 (edge st) and then work star pattern:
Rows 1 and 3 (RS): Knit.
Row 2: K1, *p3tog but do not slip sts off left needle, yo, purl the 3 sts tog once more and then slip sts off left needle, k1*. Rep from * to * until 1 st rem; end p1 (edge st).
Row 4: K1, p1, k1, *p3tog but do not slip sts off left needle, yo, purl the 3 sts tog once more and then slip sts off left needle, k1*. Rep from * to * until 3 sts rem; end p1, k1, p1 (edge st).
Rep these 4 rows (= 1 rep).

SCARF

The scarf is worked in two sections (each from the end) and then joined with a three-needle bind-off at the middle. It is knit with doubled yarn—1 strand each of the thick and thin yarns. Read through the instructions all the way to the end before you start to knit.

With 1 strand each black Fritidsgarn and black Mini Alpakka held together, CO 27 sts. The outer-most st at each side is an edge st that is slipped at the beginning of every row. Begin with 8 rows of twisted knit ribbing:

RS: (K1tbl, p1) across.

WS: Work p1tbl over purl sts as they face you and knit over knit.

After completing the ribbing, cut the black Mini Alpakka yarn and add the gray Mini Alpakka. Work in star pattern without beads for approx. 5½ in / 14 cm. Now, on every Row 3 of pattern, place beads (see page 6). Including the edge st, place beads on the 6th, 14th, and 22nd sts the first time and then, on the alternate Row 3, on the 10th and 18th sts. Knit the st after the bead has been placed. Continue the same way, with the beads staggering on each Row 3 until you've placed a total of 38 beads.

When you run out of the first ball of black Fritids-garn, change to the gray Fritidsgarn plus black Mini Alpakka. Continue in star pattern until the first ball of gray Fritidsgarn is almost finished. Place all the sts onto a holder and work the other

half of the scarf the same way except for the color sequence. In this case, the scarf starts the ribbing with 1 strand of each yarn in gray. Continue with gray Fritidsgarn and black Mini Alpakka, plus the beads until the Fritidsgarn is used up. Work the last part with black Fritidsgarn and gray Mini Alpakka and the rest of the beads.

Joining the two halves: Join with three-needle bind-off as follows: Hold the two pieces with RS facing RS and the needles with the live stitches parallel. Use an extra needle and k2tog with the first st from each needle. *K2tog with the next st on each needle, pass the first st on right needle over the new one*. Rep from * to * until 1 st rem. Cut yarn, leaving an end 8 in / 20 cm long. Draw the end through the last st. Weave in all ends neatly on WS. Gently steam press the join on WS.

KNITTING TIPS

For this pattern, begin a new yarn on Row 1 of the Star Pattern. Work the first 2 sts on the row with the previous color and then begin new color. Each half of the scarf ends on Row 4 of the Star Pattern.

Red cowl with matching ear warmer

This red cowl with soft bobble stitches is a little shorter than the blue one on page 52, so there's enough yarn to make a matching ear warmer!

DIFFICULTY LEVEL
Advanced

FINISHED MEASUREMENTS
Cowl: approx. 8 in / 20 cm high and approx. 26¾ in / 68 cm in circumference

Ear Warmer: approx. 3¼ in / 8 cm wide and approx. 20½ in / 52 cm in circumference. The bobble structure is very elastic, so this will actually fit up to Size L. You can adjust the sizing by using larger or smaller needles.

MATERIALS
Yarn:
CYCA #1 (fingering) Sandnes Garn Mini Alpakka (100% alpaca, 164 yd/150 m / 50 g), 50 g *each* colors 4219 and 4554

+

CYCA #4 (worsted, afghan, Aran) Sandnes Garn Silk Mohair (60% mohair, 25% silk, 15% wool, 306 yd/280 m / 50 g), Color 3525, 50 g

Beads:
55 beads for the cowl and 14 beads for the ear warmer, 9 mm (see Bead Tips on page 55)

NEEDLES
U.S. size 13 / 9 mm: long circular + U.S. size 17 / 12 mm for casting on loosely.

GAUGE
13 sts in bobble pattern with 3 strands of yarn held together on U.S. size 13 / 9 mm needles = approx. 4 in / 10 cm. Adjust needle size to obtain correct gauge if necessary.

INSTRUCTIONS

COWL
The cowl is worked back and forth on a long circular and finished by sewing the short ends together. Use a circular with long, pointed tips. Read through these instructions to the end before you begin knitting.

Bobble Stitch
Worked inside the edge sts. Edge st: Slip the first st of every row.

Row 1 (RS): Purl.

Row 2 (WS): Work (k1, p1, k1) into the same st, p3tog. Rep from * to * until 1 st rem, end with p1 (edge st).

Row 3: Purl.

Row 4: P3tog, work (k1, p1, k1) into same st. Rep from * to * until 1 st rem, end with p1 (edge st).

With 1 strand of each ball of yarn held together (= 3 strands), and U.S. 17 / 12 mm (if you want a loose cast-on) needle, CO 90 sts (= 88 sts + 2 edge sts for the circumference of the cowl). If you cast on with the larger needle, work the 1st row of the repeat before changing to U.S. 15 / 9 mm, with which you will work the rest of the cowl.

Begin with one pattern repeat without beads and then place beads (see page 6) on every pattern Row 3. Purl the stitch after placing bead. On the 1st bead row, the first bead is placed on the 6th st (including edge st), followed by a bead on every 8th st, so each bead lies between two bobbles. On the 2nd and 4th bead rows, place the first bead on the 2nd st (including edge st) and then on every 8th st across. On the 3rd and 5th bead rows, work as for the 1st bead row. After the 5th bead row, work 4 more rows in bobble stitch pattern. BO knitwise on next row. Make sure the bind-off is the same tension as the cast-on.

Finishing
By hand, sew the short ends together with RS facing and edges abutting. Weave in all yarn ends neatly on WS.

EAR WARMER
With 1 strand from each ball of yarn (= 3 strands held together) and U.S. 15 / 9 mm circular, CO 54 sts (= 52 sts + 2 edge sts). Purl 1 row, knit 1 row. Work Rows 1-3 of the bobble stitch pattern and place beads on Row 3. Place a bead on the 2nd st (including edge st) and then on every 8th st across. Work Row 4 of pattern and then work Rows 1-3, with beads on Row 3. Place a bead on the 6th st (including edge st), and then on every 8th st across. After this bead row, knit 1 row on WS and purl 1 row on RS. BO on the next, WS, row. Make sure the bind-off is the same tension as the cast-on.

Finishing
By hand, sew the short ends together with RS facing and edges abutting. Sew on the 14th bead if the space between the placed beads is too big. Weave in all yarn ends neatly on WS.

BEAD TIPS
We used plastic beads from a candle ring for this set. On these beads, the holes are placed outermost on one half, which allows the beads to show especially well on the right side.

Wide tube scarf with felted wool beads

Little balls made of felted wool are great for using as beads, but you have to make the bead holes yourself. Felted wool beads are, for example, especially good for a cozy and soft tube scarf, knitted in an open structure on big needles. This scarf's so wide you can actually wrap it three times around your neck if you want!

DIFFICULTY LEVEL
Intermediate

FINISHED MEASUREMENTS
The cowl is approx. 9 ¾ in / 25 cm high and 63 in / 160 cm in circumference

MATERIALS
Yarn:
CYCA #3 (DK, light worsted) Sandnes Garn Alpakka (100% alpaca, 120 yd/110 m / 50 g), 200 g Color 1099 and 100 g Color 6071

Beads and Notions:
18 felted wool beads (see next page)
darning needle and an awl or metal knitting needle

NEEDLES
U.S. size 17 / 12 mm: long circular + U.S. size 19 / 15 mm for casting on

CROCHET HOOK
U.S. sizes C-2–D-3 / 2.5-3 mm

GAUGE
7 sts in pattern on U.S. 17 / 12 mm needles = approx. 4 in / 10 cm.
Adjust needle size to obtain correct gauge if necessary.

INSTRUCTIONS

FROM FELTED WOOL TO BEADS

The wool beads for this scarf came from a square trivet made of felted wool balls sewn together, which we bought in a shop. The beads are approx. ¾ in / 2 cm in diameter. We cut the balls from the mat, and to prevent the dye from bleeding, we put them in a bowl of lukewarm vinegar water, with 2-3 tablespoons of 7% vinegar per quart/liter. We left them until they were completely saturated, and then rinsed out the vinegar and rolled them firmly between our palms until they lost their edged shape, before letting them dry in a warm place. Wherever your felted beads come from, make sure they're completely dry before you make holes in them. Begin with a large darning needle and then widen the hole with an awl or knitting needle until it's large enough for a crochet hook U.S. sizes C-2–D-3 / 2.5-3 mm or larger. Neither dental floss nor wire needles work well for placing wool beads, so you need to use a crochet hook to drop these beads onto your knit stitches.

Structure Pattern

This tube scarf is worked in the round on a circular needle in an easy structure pattern; 4 rnds = 1 repeat.
Rnd 1: (K2tog, yo) around.
Rnds 2 and 4: Knit around.
Rnd 3: (Yo, k2tog tbl) around.
In order to correctly maintain the stitch count, it is important that all rounds begin at the same place. Pm for beginning of rnd.

TUBE SCARF

The scarf is knitted with three strands of yarn held together, 2 black strands and 1 gray. Read through the instructions all the way to the end before you start to knit.

With U.S. size 19 / 15 mm needle (if you want a loose cast-on) and the 3 strands of yarn held together, CO 108 sts. Join, being careful not to twist cast-on row. Pm for beginning of rnd. Knit 1 row on same needle size as for cast-on. This rnd is not to be included in counts. The rest of the scarf is worked with the U.S. 17 / 12 mm needle.
Work around in structure pattern as described above. Place felted wool beads on the 8th, 16th, and 24th rnds = every other time you work a pattern Rnd 4. Work the first 2 sts of the rnd before you place the first bead. That prevents the bead placement from colliding with the change of rnds. All beads should be drawn in on what was a yarnover on the previous rnd. Work the stitch tbl after placing bead. There are 17 sts between each bead. On the center round of beads, place the beads so that they are centered between the beads on the 8th and 24th rnds.
Work 8 rnds (or as long as the yarn holds out) after the last bead rnd before binding off. BO so that the bound-off edge is the same tension as for the cast-on row. Weave in all yarn ends separately on WS.

Cowl and ear warmer made with Easy

When a yarn is called Easy, does that mean it's easy to knit with? In this case, yes: Easy is a thick yarn that makes knitted fabric grow quickly! The cowl in the photo is 36 in / 91 cm total—long enough to button in a variety of ways.

DIFFICULTY LEVEL
Intermediate

FINISHED MEASUREMENTS
Cowl: 11 x 36 in / 28 x 91 cm
Ear Warmer: 3½ in / 9 cm wide and approx. 19¼ in 49 cm in circumference.

MATERIALS
Yarn:
CYCA #6 (super bulky) Sandnes Garn Easy (100% wool, 55 yd/50 m / 50 g), Color 4622, 200 g for the cowl + 50 g for the ear warmer

Beads and Notions:
22 beads, 8 mm (Creativ Company)
44 + approx. 21 beads, 10 mm (Creativ Company)
7 small shank buttons to match yarn color + 7 transparent button
Sewing thread to match yarn, sewing needle
For finishing, you'll need a spray bottle, rust-free pins, and a Styrofoam plate or ironing board covered with bath towels.

NEEDLES
U.S. size 13 / 9 mm: long circular with pointed tips

GAUGE
Cowl: 12 sts in leaf pattern on U.S. size 13 / 9 mm needles = approx. 4 in / 10 cm
Ear Warmer: 11 sts in seed st on U.S. size 13 / 9 mm needles = approx. 4 in / 10 cm. Adjust needle size to obtain correct gauge if necessary.

KNITTING TIPS
When yarn needs to be spliced, you can felt it together as explained on page 9. Make sure you don't splice a thick yarn where beads will be placed.

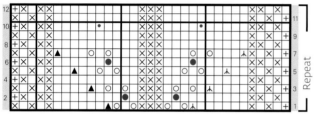

The numbers on the right side of the chart indicate right side rows; numbers on the left side of the chart indicate wrong side rows.

Symbol	Description
⊞	Edge st, sl 1 at the beginning of the row
☐	Knit on RS, purl on WS
☒	Purl on RS, knit on WS
⊙	Yo. On the WS, purl the yarnover through back loop
●	Large bead. Place the bead (see page 6) and then purl the stitch after the bead has been placed
⊡	Small bead. Place the bead (see page 6) and then purl the stitch after the bead has been placed
人	K3tog
▲	Sl 1, k2tog, psso.

INSTRUCTIONS

COWL

Read through the instructions all the way to the end before you begin to knit.

CO 29 sts and work 5 rows in seed st:
Row 1: Sl 1 (edge st), (k1, p1) to end of row.
All subsequent rows: Sl 1 (edge st) and then work purl over knit and knit over purl.
On the 6th row (WS), increase the stitch count by 4 sts; increase with pb&f (= p1tbl, p1) into the same st.

Row 6: Work 7 sts in seed st inside the edge st, * pb&f, 3 seed sts*. Rep from * to * until you've increased 4 sts total; work in seed st to end of row = 33 sts.
Now work following the charted pattern. All rows are on the chart. The yarnovers and decreases are made on the RS and the beads (see page 6) are placed on the WS.
After working 11 chart repeats, finish with 5 rows in seed st: On the 1st row of seed st (RS), decrease a total of 4 sts: Work 4 seed sts after the edge st, k2tog, 7 sts seed st, k2tog, p1, k2tog, 7 seed sts, k2tog, work in seed st to end of row = 29 sts rem. Work 4 more rows in seed st. BO in seed st.

Finishing

The leaf pattern causes knitted fabric to bias. After weaving in the yarn ends, you can dampen the cowl carefully with a steam iron; but we recommend that instead you stretch the piece by blocking it on a Styrofoam plate or an ironing board covered with heavy bath towels. Fill a spray bottle with lukewarm water and spray the cowl on the wrong side until it's damp—you don't need to saturate it. Turn it and smooth it out to the finished measurements, and then pin it closely along the edges before you spray the right side. Lightly pat the beads with a hand towel. That way, you'll avoid large water drops that might discolor the cowl. Leave until completely dry.
Sew 5 buttons along the short side (bound-off edge), about 1 in / 2.5 cm inside the outer edge. Beginning at the center, lay a flat, transparent button on the WS and sew it on with sewing thread with both buttons so there are 2¼ in / 5.5 cm between the center of each button. Also securely sew two buttons at the top of one long side, spaced 2½ in / 6 cm apart. The buttons mean that you can hold the cowl/scarf together in several ways. You don't need any buttonholes—knitting with Easy leaves "buttonholes" all over.

EAR WARMER

CO 11 sts. Work 4 rows in seed st:
Row 1: Sl 1 (edge st), (k1, p1) to end of row.
All subsequent rows: Sl 1 (edge st) and then work purl over knit and knit over purl.
*On the next row: place a bead (see page 6) on the 6th st (including edge st). Work 5 rows in seed st without beads. **Next row:** Place a bead on the 4th and 8th sts (including edge st). Work 5 rows in seed st without beads*. Rep from * to * until you've placed 21 beads or the ear warmer is desired length. BO in seed st.
Finishing: By hand, using sewing thread, sew the short ends together with ends abutted. Weave in all ends neatly on WS.

With buttons on one short end and at the top of one long side, you can wear this cowl many ways.

Scarf without a wrong side

Have you ever tried knitting a scarf with two right sides? It's so nice to have a scarf that looks great no matter which way you turn! Because the edges are worked with a type of "double knitting," the scarf doesn't roll in—so it's a scarf with two right sides that also holds its shape.

DIFFICULTY LEVEL
Advanced

FINISHED MEASUREMENTS
Purple Scarf: approx. 9¾ x 71 in / 25 x 180 cm + fringe
Old Rose Scarf: approx. 6¼ x 52 in / 15.5 x 132 cm

MATERIALS
Purple Scarf
Yarn:
CYCA #3 (DK, light worsted) Sandnes Garn Smart (100% wool, 108 yd/99 m / 50 g), Color 5226, 300 g
+
CYCA #1 (fingering) Sandnes Garn Sisu (80% wool, 20% polyamide, 191 yd/175 m / 50 g), Color 5173, 200 g

Beads:
38 large wood beads (see page 64)

NEEDLES
U.S. size 17 / 12 mm: long circular with pointed tips

CROCHET HOOK
J-10 or L-11 / 6 or 7 mm

GAUGE
10 sts in stockinette on U.S. size 17 / 12 mm needles = 4 in / 10 cm.
Adjust needle size to obtain correct gauge if necessary.

Old Rose Scarf
Yarn:
CYCA #3 (DK, light worsted) Sandnes Garn

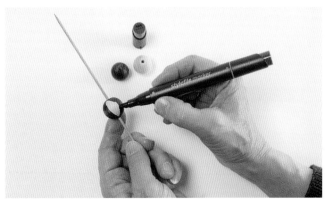

The beads we used (purchased in London) are approx. ¾ in / 18 mm in diameter, but smaller beads will also work well. If you can't find similar beads at your local craft store, try a second-hand store or look on the internet for beads you can dye. Use white wood beads and a waterproof pen (Creativ Company). Painted beads will look more matte once washed, but you can prevent this by spraying them with a clear lacquer after they've been painted.

The slip sts are crocheted inside the outermost sts. On the back, the crochet will look like small stitches.

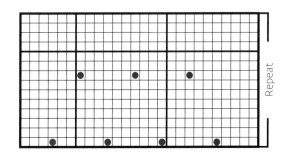

☐ Knit

◉ Bead. Knit the st after the bead has been placed

Alpakka (100% alpaca, 120 yd/110 m / 50 g), Color 4622, 150 g + about 15 yd/m Color 5031

Beads:
123 beads, 6 mm

NEEDLES
U.S. size 9 / 5.5 mm: long circular with pointed tips

CROCHET HOOK
E-4 / 3.5 mm

GAUGE
17 sts in stockinette on U.S. size 9 / 5.5 mm needles = 4 in / 10 cm.
Adjust needle size to obtain correct gauge if necessary.

INSTRUCTIONS

STOCKINETTE WITH TWO RIGHT SIDES
The scarf is knitted back and forth with an even number of stitches. The first st is always worked as k1 or k1tbl; the last st is slipped.

Double Knitting
K1. Bring the yarn forward, between the st you just knit and the next st, sl the next st purlwise, take yarn back between the sts. Rep from * to * across.
NOTE: When counting stitches and rows, only the stitches and rows on the front side are counted. All the beads are placed on the front side of the scarf.

PURPLE SCARF
With 2 strands of yarn (= 1 strand Smart + 1 strand Sisu) held together, CO 50 sts. Work in stockinette with two right sides (double knitting) as explained above. The first st of every row is knit. Work 8 rows without beads. Don't forget that only the rows and stitches on the front side are counted and that beads are placed only on front side stitches.
1st Bead Row: *Place a bead (see page 6) on the 6th and 20th sts. Knit the st after the bead has been placed. Work 7 rows without beads.
2nd Bead Row: Place a bead on the 13th st. Work 7 rows without beads*. Rep from * to * until you've placed 38 beads total.
End the scarf with 8 rows without beads. BO on the back side, by working k2tog across and binding off at the same time by passing the first st over the second on right needle.
The scarf has 13 fringes at each end. Each fringe consists of a yarn bundle, 19¾-21¾ in / 50-55 cm long, with 8 strands from each ball of yarn in each bundle. With the crochet hook, draw the center of the bundle through the knitted edge to the back

side so you have an open loop there. Twist the loop a little so that the strands lie parallel. Use your fingers to pull the long yarn ends through the loop. Tighten for a fine loop knot. Instead of weaving in the yarn ends at the beginning and end of the scarf, you can add them to the outer-most fringe knots. When all the fringes are in place, even them out, trimming them with scissors. The finished fringes on the sample shown here are approx. 8¾ in / 22 cm long.

OLD ROSE SCARF
This scarf is worked as for the purple scarf. Read through the instructions all the way to the end before you start to knit. The beads on the

sample shown here were taken from some costume jewelry.

CO 52 sts and work in stockinette with two right sides as described above. On this scarf, the first st on each row is worked as k1tbl. The last st on each row is always slipped. Work 15 rows without beads. Now place beads (see page 6) as shown on the chart. Work 14 rows without beads after the last bead row. BO and neatly weave in yarn ends.

With the gray-purple yarn, crochet all around the scarf in slip st: hold the yarn on the back side of the knitting while you work in slip st inside the outermost st along the edges on the right side of the scarf. Weave in rem ends.

Necklace

This jeweled collar is easy to knit. You don't need to increase or decrease—just work back and forth on circular needles of varying sizes. You can finish it with a button and loop, tie it with a narrow silk ribbon, or use a brooch. Both versions have beads from old costume jewelry—creative recycling!

DIFFICULTY LEVEL
Intermediate

FINISHED MEASUREMENTS
Gray Necklace: approx. 1½ in / 4 cm wide and approx. 14¼ in / 36 cm on the inner edge of neck and approx. 21¼ in / 54 cm along the outer edge. The stitch count is a multiple of 3 + an edge st at each side.
Purple Necklace: approx. 2¼ in / 5.5 cm wide and approx. 13½ in / 34 cm on the inner edge of neck and approx. 25½ in / 65 cm along the outer edge. The stitch count is a multiple of 4 + 1 + an edge st at each side.

MATERIALS
Gray Necklace
Yarn:
CYCA #4 (worsted, afghan, Aran) Sandnes Garn Line (53% cotton, 33% other, 14% linen, 120 yd/110 m / 50 g), Color 5870, 50 g
Beads:
86 beads, 6 mm

NEEDLES
U.S. sizes 4, 6, 7, and 8 / 3.5, 4, 4.5, and 5 mm: circulars

CROCHET HOOK
G-6 / 4 mm

Purple Necklace
Yarn:
CYCA #3 (DK, light worsted) Garn Studio (Drops) Cotton Viscose (54% cotton, 46% viscose, 120 yd/110 m / 50 g), Color 30, 50 g

Beads and Notions:
68 beads, 5 mm
1 button, approx. ½ in / 12 mm

NEEDLES

U.S. sizes 4, 6, 7, 8, and 9 / 3.5, 4, 4.5, 5, and 5.5 mm: circulars

CROCHET HOOK

E-4 / 3.5 mm

GAUGE

20 sts in stockinette on U.S. size 6 / 3.5 mm needles = 4 in / 10 cm.
Adjust needle size to obtain correct gauge if necessary.

INSTRUCTIONS

GRAY COLLAR WITH AN EASY STRUCTURE PATTERN

Easy Structure Pattern
The first st of every row is slipped as an edge st. Work as follows inside the edge sts:
Row 1 (RS): K2, *yo, k3, pass the first of the 3 sts over the next two*. Rep from * to * until 2 sts rem, end k2.
Rows 2 and 4: Purl and, *at the same time*, add beads: place 1 bead (see page 6) on each yarnover of the previous row; place the yarnover back on left needle and purl it as for the other sts on the row.
Row 3: K1, *k3, pass the first of the 3 sts over the other 2, yo*. Rep from * to * until 3 sts rem, end k3.
Rep these 4 rows (= 1 repeat).

Do you like gray? A gray necklace goes with pretty much everything! If you close it with a brooch, you'll have a new piece of jewelry every time you change the brooch. Or use a small Norwegian silver brooch—in Norway, so many lovely pieces of jewelry for traditional folk costumes only come out on 17 May (Norway's national holiday), which is a shame!

Begin with the U.S. 4 / 3.5 mm circular. CO 92 sts. Knit 2 rows and then work Rows 1-2 of the pattern repeat as described above, with beads on Row 2. Change to U.S. 6 / 4 mm circular. Work Rows 3-4 of the pattern, with beads on Row 4. Change to U.S. 7 / 4.5 mm circular. Work Rows 1-2 of the pattern repeat as described above, with beads on Row 2. Change to U.S. 8 / 5 mm circular. Purl 1 row on RS. BO knitwise on next, WS, row. Work 1-2 rows of sc on each short end (try on the collar around your neck to see how many rows are needed); fasten off ends.

PURPLE COLLAR WITH STAR STITCH PATTERN

Star Stitch Pattern
The first st of every row is slipped as an edge st. Work as follows inside the edge sts:
Rows 1 and 3 (RS): Knit across, also placing beads (see page 6) on this row. After placing a bead, knit the stitch with the bead.
Row 2: K1, *p3tog, but do not slip sts off left needle, yo, p3tog once more, and slip sts off needle, k1*. Rep from * to * to last st and end with p1 (edge st).
Row 4: K1, p1, k1, *p3tog, but do not slip sts off left needle, yo, p3tog once more, and slip sts off needle, k1*. Rep from * to * to until 3 sts rem; end with p1, k1, p1 (edge st).
Rep these 4 rows (= 1 repeat).

With U.S. 4 / 3.5 mm needle, CO 95 sts (= 93 sts + 2 edge sts which are slipped at the beginning of every row). Knit 2 rows and then work Rows 1-2 of Star Stitch Pattern without beads. Change to U.S. 6 / 4 mm circular. Work Rows 3-4 of Star Stitch Pattern. Next, work Row 1 and place

YARN TIP
Viscose is a very slippery yarn, so make sure it doesn't slide out while you place the beads on the stitches.

a bead on every 4th st of this row.

Change to US. 7 / 4 mm circular. Work Rows 2-3, with a bead on every 4th st of Row 3, with the first bead placed on the 6th st (including edge st).

Change to U.S. 8 / 5 mm circular. Work Rows 4 and 1 of Star Stitch Pattern. Place 1 bead on every 4th st of Row 1.

Change to U.S. 9 / 5.5 mm circular. Knit 2 rows, 1 row on WS and 1 on RS. BO knitwise on next, WS, row.

Finish by crocheting a closely spaced row of picots around the collar. Work with RS facing. Begin at the top on one of the short sides.

Picots: *Ch 3, 1 sc into first st of ch, 1 sl st in next st*. Rep from * to * around the outer edge of the collar and over other short end. With this pattern, there is a picot in each of the stitches around the outer edge. To round the edges of the lower corners, make an extra picot in the corner st.

Sew the button to the top left side of the collar. On the opposite side, crochet a button loop to fit button. Weave in all ends neatly on WS.

Poncho

Wonderfully soft and warm. This simple garment is one of those that everyone should own. It's easy to make but offers endless ways to wear it every day, or at parties. This one, knitted with Silk Mohair and Mini Alpakka and beads down the shoulders, will liven up every outfit.

DIFFICULTY LEVEL
Advanced

FINISHED MEASUREMENTS
The length of this poncho (that is, the width of the knitted fabric) is approx. 23¾ in / 60 cm from the shoulder seam to the lower edge. The width (that is, the length of the knitted fabric) is approx. 53¼ in / 135 cm. If you want a larger or smaller poncho, you can cast on more/fewer stitches, or knit it longer/shorter. The beads align over a section about 16½ in / 42 cm long. The beads are placed where the poncho will be seamed (at the shoulder seam). The poncho also has beads around the neck.

MATERIALS
Yarn:
CYCA #1 (fingering) Sandnes Garn Mini Alpakka (100% alpaca, 164 yd/150 m / 50 g), Color 1088, 300 g
+
CYCA #4 (worsted, afghan, Aran) Sandnes Garn Silk Mohair (60% mohair, 25% silk, 15% wool, 306 yd/280 m / 50 g), Color 1099, 150 g

Beads:
38-40 beads, black/gray harmony resin beads, or Kongomix-beads, approx. 10 mm (Creativ Company)

NEEDLES
U.S. size 9 / 5.5 mm: long circular

GAUGE
14 sts in garter stitch welt pattern with 2 strands of yarn held together on U.S. size 9 / 5.5 mm needles = 4 in / 10 cm.
Adjust needle size to obtain correct gauge if necessary.

INSTRUCTIONS
The poncho is worked back and forth and seamed.

Garter Stitch Welt
NOTE: Always knit the first st of every row as an edge st.
Row 1: Knit.
Row 2: Do not turn, but begin working from the right side with a new strand of doubled yarn.
Row 3: Knit with the yarn from previous row.
Row 4: Do not turn, but begin on the right side and work with the yarn hanging at side.
Row 5: Knit with the yarn from previous row. *At the same time*, place a bead on the 3rd st (see page 6) = k2, place bead on 3rd st.
Rep Rows 2-5 = 4-row repeat.

PONCHO
With 1 strand of each yarn held together, CO 80 sts. Work back and forth in Garter Stitch Welt (see above). Rows 2-5 are repeated throughout, with beads placed on each Row 5, until you've used approx. 25 beads (= 16½ in / 42 cm). For the neck opening, continue in Garter Stitch Welt, placing beads on the last row of every 3rd rep (= every 12 rows). When you've used 12-14 beads for the neck, continue in pattern without beads for approx. 16½ in / 42 cm.

Finishing
BO loosely. Cut yarn, leaving an end about 31½ in / 80 cm long; draw end through last st. Use the yarn end to hand sew the seam on the wrong side along the bead edge. Weave in all ends neatly on WS.

Shawl with faceted beads

Have you been longing for a soft and comfy shawl? This shawl is great for throwing over your shoulders when it's cool, and it also doubles as a scarf! One side has eyelets, so you can draw a ribbon through the lace and then wear the shawl as a cape. Alternatively, you can wear the shawl over your shoulders and tie it with the ribbon at the center front.

DIFFICULTY LEVEL
Advanced

FINISHED MEASUREMENTS
When the shawl is laid flat, it measures approx.
15¾ x 57 in / 40 x 145 cm. If you wear it as a scarf, it will narrow in width and stretch out lengthwise to 71 in / 180 cm.

MATERIALS
Yarn:
CYCA #1 (fingering) Sandnes Garn Mini Alpakka (100% alpaca, 164 yd/150 m / 50 g), Color 6081, 100 g
+

CYCA #4 (worsted, afghan, Aran) Sandnes Garn Silk Mohair (60% mohair, 25% silk, 15% wool, 306 yd/280 m / 50 g), Color 1076, 50 g

Beads:
246 metallic gray faceted beads, 5 x 6 mm (Creativ Company)

NEEDLES
U.S. size 13 / 9 mm: circular or long straight needles

GAUGE
10 sts in lace pattern with 2 strands of yarn held together on U.S. size 13 / 9 mm needles =
4 in / 10 cm.
Adjust needle size to obtain correct gauge if necessary.

INSTRUCTIONS

The shawl is worked back and forth with 1 strand of each yarn held together throughout.

CO 41 sts and knit 5 rows, back and forth. The 6th row is the WS and is purled. Now work following the charted pattern on next page. Rep Rows 1-16 12 times total before repeating Rows 17-18 once. Finish with 5 rows garter st (= knit all rows) and then BO knitwise on next, WS, row. Weave in all yarn ends neatly on WS.

The numbers on the right side of the chart indicate right side rows; numbers on the left side of the chart indicate wrong side rows. Rep Rows 1-16.

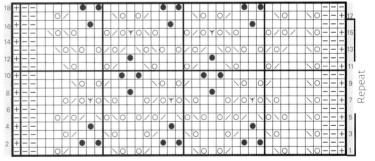

⊞ Edge st, sl 1 at the beginning of the row

☐ Knit on RS, purl on WS

⊟ Knit on all rows

⊙ Yo. On the WS, purl the yarnover through back loop

⊙ Place the bead (see page 6) and then purl the stitch after the bead has been placed

◺ Sl 1, k1, psso (or ssk)

◿ K2tog

Υ Sl 2 tog knitwise, k1, p2sso (centered double decrease)

Scarves

When we say "scarf," what image comes to mind? A piece of cotton or silk fabric? We asked ourselves why all scarves must be made from fabric and of course it isn't necessarily so. It's obvious that you can knit a scarf!

DIFFICULTY LEVEL
Intermediate

FINISHED MEASUREMENTS
Black Scarf with Bling: approx. 13¾ x 13¾ in / 35 x 35 cm
Purple Scarf: approx. 17¾ x 17¾ in / 45 x 45 cm

MATERIALS
Yarn:
Black Scarf with Bling:
CYCA #3 (DK, light worsted) Sandnes Garn Al-pakka (100% alpaca, 120 yd/110 m / 50 g), Color 1088, 50 g
+
CYCA #4 (worsted, afghan, Aran) Sandnes Garn Silk Mohair (60% mohair, 25% silk, 15% wool, 306 yd/280 m / 50 g), Color 1099, 50 g
+

CYCA #0 (lace) Garn Studio Drops Lace (70% alpaca, 30% silk, 437 yd/400 m / 50 g), color 8903, 50 g
+
CYCA #0 (lace/thread) Du Store Alpakka Bling Effekttråd (100% Polyester, 382 yd/349 m / 50 g), Color 3002, 1 spool

Beads:
23 beads, 8 mm (Creativ Company)

Yarn:
Purple Scarf:
CYCA #3 (DK, light worsted) Sandnes Garn Smart (100% wool, 108 yd/99 m / 50 g), Color 5229, 50 g
+
CYCA #4 (worsted, afghan, Aran) Sandnes Garn Silk Mohair (60% mohair, 25% silk, 15% wool, 306 yd/280 m / 50 g), 50 g *each* of colors 5153 and 4853

Beads: 80-100 faceted beads, 4-12 mm (Creativ Company)

Tie the scarves together, and secure them with a brooch or a decorative pin.

NEEDLES
U.S. size 15 / 10 mm: circular with long, pointed tips (both versions)

GAUGE
Black Scarf with Bling: 10 sts in seed st = 4 in / 10 cm.
Purple Scarf: 8 sts in seed st = approx. 4 in / 10 cm. Adjust needle size to obtain correct gauge if necessary.

INSTRUCTIONS

BLACK SCARF WITH BLING
This scarf is worked with yarn from 4 balls of yarn. The effect yarn and the beads make it more than a typical scarf. A little "glam" never hurts, even for everyday wear! This scarf is very soft and flexible, so you can wear it as a collar, as a detached high turtleneck, or fold it into a triangle and knot it to wear with the pointed tip forward.

The scarf is worked back and forth in seed st. Cast on and bind off omitting the Bling effect yarn. The rest of the scarf is worked with all 4 yarns held together.

With the alpaca, silk-mohair, and lace yarns held together, CO 37 sts (= 35 sts + 2 edge sts). Always slip the 1st st of each row as an edge st. Add the bling effect yarn = 4 strands held together. Between the edge sts, work (k1, p1) across. On subsequent rows, work purl over knit and knit over purl. Place beads (see page 6) beginning on the 7th row. If the sequins on the bling yarn are too large for the bead hole, lay the yarn behind the fabric when placing the bead. After placing the bead on the stitch, knit or purl the st in pattern. Place the beads randomly or as in our model:

Row 7: Work 6 sts (including edge) st, place 1 bead, work 11 sts between the next 2 beads, work to end of row (= 3 beads total placed). Work 5 rows without beads.

Row 13: Work 12 sts (including edge st), place 1 bead, work 11 sts and then place bead, complete row (2 beads placed on row).

Continue as est, alternating bead rows with 3 and 2 beads per row, and 5 rows between each bead row. When scarf measures approx. 13¾ in / 35 cm, cut Bling yarn and BO in seed st. Weave in all ends *separately* on WS. If it is difficult to weave in the Bling yarn through the knitting when fastening off, cut off the sequins with sharp, pointed scissors before weaving in this yarn.

PURPLE SCARF
CO 37 sts with one strand from each ball of yarn (= 3 strands held together) and work the purple scarf as for the black one, placing the pink/purple beads randomly.

Soul warmer (shrug)

Some call this garment a soul warmer, while others consider it a shawl with sleeves. No matter what you call it, it's a garment you can wear often! With beads on the lower edges of the sleeves, this shrug can enhance any simple outfit. It's nice to have over a thin party dress, or over the shoulders when early autumn evenings start to get cool. The shrug is worked back and forth, without any increasing or decreasing—the sizing is achieved by changing needle sizes.

DIFFICULTY LEVEL
Advanced

FINISHED MEASUREMENTS
When the shrug is laid flat, it is 55 in / 140 cm long, but when you put it on, it stretches by about 4 in / 10 cm. As measured down center back, the shawl is approx. 19¾ in / 50 cm wide (18½ in / 47 cm + edges). The bead section at the cuffs is 16½ in / 42 cm wide before seaming and approx. 1½ in / 4 cm high.

MATERIALS
Yarn:
CYCA #4 (worsted, afghan, Aran) Sandnes Garn Line (53% cotton, 33% other, 14% linen, 120 yd/ 110 m / 50 g), Color 5870, 300 g

Beads:
70 resin beads, 10 mm, black/gray harmony (Creativ Company)

NEEDLES
U.S. sizes 7, 8, 9, 10, 10½, and 11 / 4.5, 5, 5.5, 6, 6.5 and 7 mm: long circulars

The garter stitch edging around the shoulders has more stitches than the garter stitch edging at the lower edge of shrug. That makes the shawl lie more smoothly around the shoulders than it would if the edges were identical.

CROCHET HOOK
D-3 / 3 mm

GAUGE
Lower edge of sleeves: 20 sts in garter st =
4 in / 10 cm.
At center back: 16 sts in garter st = 4 in / 10 cm.
Adjust needle size to obtain correct gauge if necessary.

INSTRUCTIONS
The shrug is worked back and forth in one piece, from cuff to cuff. It is later seamed by hand at the lower edges of the sleeves. The crossed stitches form an easy structure pattern.

Crossed Stitches
Always slip the 1st st of every row as an edge st. The crossed stitch pattern is worked within the edge sts.
Row 1 (WS): Purl.
Row 2 (RS): P1, *into 2nd st, k1tbl but do not slip st from needle, k1tbl into 1st st and then slip both sts off left needle at the same time, p1*. Rep from * to * across.
Row 3: K1, *purl the 2nd st, but do not slip st from needle, purl the 1st st and then slip both sts off left needle at the same time, k1*. Rep from * to * across.
Row 4: Knit.
Rep Rows 1-4 (4 rows = 1 repeat).

SHRUG
Read through the instructions all the way to the end before you begin knitting.
With U.S. 7 / 4.5 mm circular, CO 75 sts (= 73 sts + 2 edge sts). Knit 5 rows. Begin Crossed Stitch pattern as described above. Place beads (see page 6) on the 4th row in pattern for the first 3 repeats. On the first and third bead rows, place a bead on the 5th st (including edge st) and then place a bead on every 6th st. Work the st as knit or twisted knit after placing bead.
On the center bead row, place the first bead on the 8th st (including edge st) and then on every 6th st across. After these 3 bead rows, continue in Crossed Stitch pattern without beads. Change needle sizes as follows:
Work 10 rep total on U.S. 7 / 4.5 mm circular.
Work 7 rep total on U.S. 8 / 5 mm circular.
Work 6 rep total on U.S. 9 / 5.5 mm circular.
Work 4 rep total on U.S. 10 / 6 mm circular.
Work 4 rep total on U.S. 10½ / 6.5 mm circular.
Work 13 rep (center section) total on U.S. 11 / 7 mm circular.
If you want a longer or shorter shawl, you can change the number of repeats in the center section.

After completing the 13 center section repeats, work back the same way, changing needles to smaller sizes. There are a total of 75 repeats, with beads on the three lower repeats when you have completed 7 rep with U.S. 7 / 4.5 needles. The beads are placed as for the first cuff at the beginning of shrug. End with Rows 1-2 of the repeat after the third row of beads. Knit 4 rows. BO knitwise on WS.

Finishing
Weave in all yarn ends neatly on WS. The Line yarn is easy to split into plies. If you do that, the weaving in won't be as clumpy. At both ends, hand stitch, the lower 11¾ in / 30 cm with back stitch—with RS facing RS and an approx. ¼ in / .75 cm seam allowance. Seam with half the yarn plies as the thread.
Work the garter stitch edging around the shawl, from sleeve seam to sleeve seam. With a long circular U.S. size 8 / 5 mm, work each side separately.
Hold the edge of the shawl with the RS facing you and the yarn behind the edge. Use the crochet hook to catch the yarn for the new sts through to the RS. Place each st onto the circular after picking up. On our model, we picked up 76 sts along the lower edge and 106 sts along the shoulder edge.
Knit 4 rows back and forth, with the first row on WS. BO knitwise, with U.S. size 8 / 5 mm needle on WS. Make sure that the binding off does not draw in. Seam the ends of the garter st edges with the sleeve seams.

NEEDLE AND BEAD TIPS
Metal needles with blunt, smooth points don't work well with Line yarn and crossed stitches. We recommend a circular with wooden tips instead. We used 3 packets of black/gray Resin beads for our version. If you want single-color beads, a good alternative is the gray Kongomix (Creativ Company).

HIGH FIVE FOR THE WEATHER

Wrist warmers and mittens aren't just warm—knitted with beads, they double as jewelry to dress up your entire outfit!

Stylish garter stitch wrist warmers

These wrist warmers will dress up every type of outfit. You won't need any other jewelry when you are wearing these.

DIFFICULTY LEVEL
Easy

FINISHED MEASUREMENTS
These wrist warmers are very elastic and will fit most wrists. They measure approx. 8¾ in / 22 cm at the bottom edge with beads and are about 5¼ in / 13 cm long. If you want larger or smaller wrist warmers, you can make the section before/after the bead area shorter/longer.

MATERIALS
Yarn:
CYCA #3 (DK, light worsted) Sandnes Garn Alpakka (100% alpaca, 120 yd/110 m / 50 g), Color 1099, 50 g

Beads:
98 beads, gray metallic luxury wax beads, 5-6 mm (Creativ Company)

NEEDLES
U.S. size 4 / 3.5 mm: circular

GAUGE
20 sts in garter st = 4 in / 10 cm.
Adjust needle size to obtain correct gauge if necessary.

INSTRUCTIONS
Read through the instructions all the way to the end before you start to knit. The wrist warmers are worked back and forth and seamed afterwards. Make both alike.

CO 25 sts (the length of the cuff). Knit back and forth in garter st for approx. 2 in / 5 cm. Place beads as follows: Place a bead (see page 6) but do not knit the stitch; work the st as k1tbl on the next row.
Row 1: K2, place bead on the 3rd st (do not knit st), knit to end of row.

Row 2: Knit, working the st with the bead as k1tbl.

Row 3: K3, place bead on the 3rd st, k1, place bead on the 5th st, knit to end of row = 2 beads on the row.

Row 4: Knit, working beaded sts as k1tbl.

Continue, placing 1 more bead on every other row (rows 5, 7, 9, etc), on every other st.

When there are 6 beads per row and you have knitted to the end of the row, begin short rows:

K12 (back to the beads), turn and knit back. Turn and knit to to end of row. Continue the same way in short rows until there are 7 beads on the row. Now you are at the center of the bead pattern. Instead of placing 1 more bead on every other row, you will add 1 bead fewer on alternate rows. When there are 6 beads, work one more short row. Now place 1 bead fewer on alternate rows until there is only 1 bead on the row. End by working 2 in / 5 cm garter st without beads. BO loosely. Cut yarn, leaving an 11¾ in / 30 cm end. Draw end through last st. Seam the bound-off and cast-on edges using the yarn end. Weave in all ends neatly on WS.

Dual garter stitch wrist warmers and ear warmer

When you knit with two strands of yarn (one at each side of the knitted fabric), and twist them only on alternate rows as done here, it will look as if you've worked two knit rows and two purl rows, even if you actually knitted the whole time. This technique produces a very elastic knitted piece.

DIFFICULTY LEVEL
Advanced

FINISHED MEASUREMENTS
Wrist Warmers: Approx. 5¾ in / 14 cm long and about 8 in / 20 cm in circumference.
Ear Warmer: Approx. 4 in / 10 cm wide and approx. 17¼ in / 44 cm in circumference.

MATERIALS
Yarn:
Color 1: CYCA #3 (DK, light worsted) Sandnes Peer Gynt (100% wool, 98 yd/90 m / 50 g), Color 4228, 50 g

Color 2: CYCA #3 (DK, light worsted) Sandnes Garn Alpakka (100% alpaca, 120 yd/110 m / 50 g), Color 4308, 50 g

Beads:
115 red luxury wax beads, (Creativ Company) = 30 10 mm beads for the wrist warmers and 70-85 5 mm beads for the ear warmer

NEEDLES
U.S. size 4 / 3.5 mm: 16 in / 40 cm circular

GAUGE
16 sts in dual garter st = 4 in / 10 cm.
Adjust needle size to obtain correct gauge if necessary.

WRIST WARMERS

With Color 1, CO 35 sts (the length of the cuffs). Knit 2 rows.
With Color 2, knit 2 rows.
Continue, alternating 2 rows each colors 1 and 2 until piece measures approx. 2 in / 5 cm.
Now work the first stockinette panel with beads, with Color 2:
Knit 1 row.
Purl 1 row.
Knit 1 row with beads: K5, place bead on every 6th st (= 5 beads across row), end with k5.
Purl 1 row.
With Color 1, knit 4 rows.
Work another stockinette section with Color 2 and beads (5 beads) as before. Continue in garter st, alternating 2 rows each colors 1 and 2 until wrist warmer measures approx. 6¾ in / 17 cm or it fits around wrist.
BO loosely. Cut yarn, leaving a 15¾ in / 40 cm end. Draw end through last st. Seam bound-off edge to cast-on edge as described in note below. Weave in all ends neatly on WS.
NOTE: Make sure that you seam the wrist warmers so that you have one for the right hand and other for the left hand.
Work as follows:
Fold the wrist warmer so that the short garter stitch sections meet. Seam approx. 1¼ in / 3 cm down the edge. Leave an opening about 1½ in / 4 cm long for the thumb, and then seam the rest. Weave in all ends neatly on WS.

EAR WARMER

The ear warmer has only one stockinette section and one row of beads all around the head. It is worked back and forth lengthwise and seamed at center back.
CO 90 sts and work the first section as for the first section on the wrist warmers (approx. 2 in / 5 cm). Work the stockinette and beads panel as for wrist warmers (1 bead on every 6th st = 15 beads). With Color 1 knit 4 rows in garter st. Continue in garter stitch, alternating 2 rows each of Colors 1 and 2 for about 1 in / 2.5 cm (knit more rows if you want a wider band).
BO loosely. Cut yarn, leaving a 9¾ in / 25 cm end. Draw end through last st and then use it to seam center back. Weave in all ends neatly on WS.

Easy lace wrist warmers

These wrist warmers are very easy to knit, and are very warming, too.

DIFFICULTY LEVEL
Easy

FINISHED MEASUREMENTS
These wrist warmers are Size S. Length approx. 5¼ in / 13 cm long and about 6¾ in / 17 cm in circumference. If you want a wider model, just cast on more stitches outside of the 13-st bead panel.

MATERIALS
Yarn:
CYCA #1 (fingering) Sandnes Garn Mini Alpakka (100% alpaca, 164 yd/150 m / 50 g), Color 1042, 50 g

Beads:
48 plastic mother-of-pearl beads, approx. 4 mm (Creativ Company)

NEEDLES
U.S. size 2.5 / 3 mm: set of 5 dpn

GAUGE
24 sts in stockinette st = 4 in / 10 cm. Adjust needle size to obtain correct gauge if necessary.

INSTRUCTIONS
The wrist warmers are worked in the round on 4 dpn. For placing beads, see page 6. Make both wrist warmers alike.

Work rep a total of 8 times

☐ Knit
☒ Purl
⊙ Yo
◉ Knit with bead placed on st (see page 6 on bead placement).

◣ K2tog tbl
◢ K2tog

WRIST WARMERS (MAKE 2 ALIKE)

CO 40 sts. Divide sts onto dpn. Join, being careful not to twist cast-on row. Pm for beginning of rnd. Knit 8 rnds. On the 9th rnd, divide the sts as follows: 9 sts on dpn 1, 9 sts on dpn 2, 13 sts on dpn 3 (lace pattern), and 9 sts on dpn 4. Knit around to dpn 3 which will be worked following the charted 13-st pattern. All the sts on dpn 1, 2, and 4 are knitted.

Continue around, repeating the 13-st lace and bead pattern 8 times (or to desired length). Finish with 3 knit rnds and then BO loosely.

Cut yarn, leaving an 8 in / 20 cm end. Draw end through last st. Weave in all ends neatly on WS.

Diagonal rib wrist warmers

Here's a somewhat different pair of wrist warmers with beads on diagonal ribbing.

DIFFICULTY LEVEL
Intermediate

FINISHED MEASUREMENTS
Approx. 4¾ in / 12 cm long and about 7½ in / 19 cm in circumference. The diagonal ribbing makes these accessories very elastic.

MATERIALS
Yarn:
CYCA #3 (DK, light worsted) Sandnes Garn Alpakka (100% alpaca, 120 yd/110 m / 50 g), Color 6544, 50 g

Beads:
24 turquoise Kongomix beads, approx. 10 mm (Creativ Company)

NEEDLES
U.S. size 4 / 3.5 mm: set of 5 dpn

GAUGE
22 sts in ribbing = 4 in / 10 cm.
Adjust needle size to obtain correct gauge if necessary.

INSTRUCTIONS
The diagonal stripe effect is produced by staggering the ribbing. Work 3 rnds of k2, p2 ribbing and then shift the rib 1 st to the left on every 4th rnd. For bead placement, see page 6. The wrist warmers are worked in the round on 4 dpn. Make both wrist warmers alike.

94

CO 40 sts and divide sts onto dpn. Join, being careful not to twist sts. Pm for beginning of rnd.

NOTE: The chart shows the first 16 sts of the round with beads. After completing charted sts, continue around in ribbing without beads over rem 24 sts.

Work 1 rnd in k2, p2 ribbing without beads. On the next rnd, place a bead, see chart. Work 1 rnd without beads before you shift the pattern 1 st to the left; continue, following chart. After completing charted rows, BO loosely. Cut yarn, leaving an 8 in / 20 cm end. Draw end through rem st. Weave in all ends neatly on WS.

The chart shows the first 16 sts of the round

☐   Knit

☒   Purl

◉   Purl st with bead. Place the bead and then purl the st

Wrist warmers to dress up your jeans outfit

Elegant, light, and lofty—embellishments for your outfit. It won't take you much time to knit these wrist warmers.

DIFFICULTY LEVEL
Intermediate

FINISHED MEASUREMENTS
Approx. 6¼ in / 16 cm long and about 7½ in / 19 cm in circumference.

MATERIALS
Yarn:
CYCA #1 (fingering) Sandnes Garn Mini Alpakka (100% alpaca, 164 yd/150 m / 50 g), Color 5575, 50 g
+
CYCA #4 (worsted, afghan, Aran) Sandnes Garn Silk Mohair (60% mohair, 25% silk, 15% wool, 306 yd/280 m / 50 g), Color 6863, 50 g

Beads:
46-50 beads, approx. 5 mm (ours came from a necklace)

NEEDLES
U.S. size 8 / 5 mm: circular

GAUGE
15 sts in pattern with a strand of each yarn held together = 4 in / 10 cm.
Adjust needle size to obtain correct gauge if necessary.

INSTRUCTIONS
Read through the instructions all the way to the end before you start to knit. These wrist warmers are worked back and forth on a circular and seamed in finishing.

Placing Beads

The beads on the lower edge of the cuffs are knitted in on Row 3: K2, place bead on the 3rd st (see page 6), slip st back to left needle and knit it. K1, place bead on the next st and then knit st. Continue, placing a bead on every other st across until 2 sts rem, end k2 = 13 beads total.

The vertical rows of beads are knitted in on the 15th st of every Row 3 of pattern.

WRIST WARMERS

Holding a strand of each yarn together, CO 29 sts (= circumference of cuff).

Row 1: Knit the first 2 and last 2 sts. Purl all rem sts between edge sts.

Row 2: K2, M1 between the 2nd and 3rd sts, k4, k2tog, k2tog tbl, k4, M1, k1, M1, k4, k2tog, k2tog tbl, k4, M1, k2.

Row 3: Knit, placing beads as described on page 96.

Row 4: Work as for Row 1.

Row 5: Work as for Row 2.

Row 6: Work as for Row 3.

Rep Rows 1-6 until wrist warmer is desired length. BO on a Row 3 without beads. Cut yarn, leaving an 11¾ in / 30 cm end; draw end through last st. Use end to seam cast-on and bound-off edges.

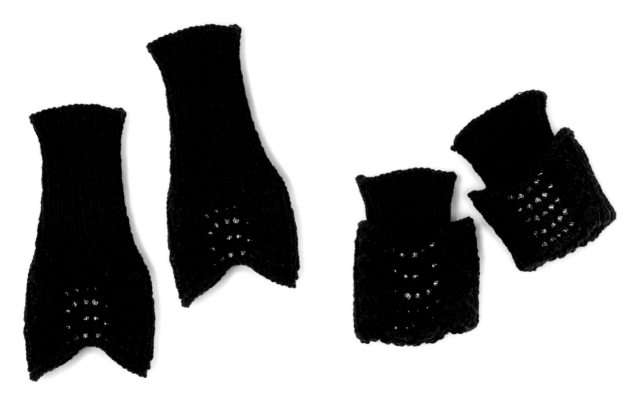

Black cuffs with bead motifs

These cuffs have a ribbed section and a bead section. The bead panels can be folded over the sleeve cuff on a jacket or coat. The cuffs can also be worn as extra-long wrist warmers when they're left full length.

DIFFICULTY LEVEL
Intermediate

FINISHED MEASUREMENTS
These cuffs are approx. 8 in / 20 cm long and approx. 8 in / 20 cm in circumference. The bead panels, which can be folded back, measure 2¾-3¼ in / 7-8 cm. The ribbing is approx. 4¾ in / 12 cm long.

MATERIALS
Yarn:
CYCA #3 (DK, light worsted) Sandnes Garn Merinoull (100% Merino wool, 114 yd/104 m / 50 g), Color 1099, 50 g

Buttons:
50 transparent beads, approx. 3-4 mm (these came from a bracelet)

NEEDLES
U.S. size 4 / 3.5 mm: set of 5 dpn

GAUGE
22 sts in ribbing = 4 in / 10 cm.
Adjust needle size to obtain correct gauge if necessary.

INSTRUCTIONS
For bead placement, see page 6. These cuffs are worked in the round on double-pointed needles.

CO 44 sts and divide sts onto dpn. Join, being careful not to twist cast-on row; pm for beginning of rnd. Knit 1 rnd. Now work following the chart on the next page. Rep the charted rows 5 times in length (until the piece is approx. 2¾-3¼ in / 7-8 cm long. After completing charted rows, knit

2 rnds. Purl 1 rnd and, *at the same time*, decrease 1 st on each dpn = 4 sts decreased and 40 sts rem. Continue in k1, p1 ribbing until ribbing is approx. 4¾ in / 12 cm long. BO loosely in ribbing. Cut yarn, leaving an end 8 in / 20 cm long; draw end through last st. Weave in all ends neatly on WS.

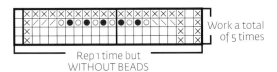

Work a total of 5 times

Rep 1 time but
WITHOUT BEADS

☐ Knit

☒ Purl

◎ Yarnover

● Knit with bead = place bead and then knit st

◩ K2tog tbl

◪ K2tog

Ruffled wrist warmers

With crocheted ruffles and beads combined with easy ribbing, these cuffs are pretty and look more difficult than they are. Plus, they're great to wear on cold days! You can wear them with the ruffles down over your fingers or over a sweater cuff with the ruffles upwards.

DIFFICULTY LEVEL
Advanced

FINISHED MEASUREMENTS
The wrist warmers are approx. 4½ in / 11.5 cm long. The ribbing is approx. 6 in / 15 cm in circumference. The ribbing is very elastic so these cuffs should fit almost anyone. If you want to adjust the sizing, you'll need an even number of stitches.

MATERIALS
Yarn:
CYCA #3 (DK, light worsted) Sandnes Garn Smart (100% wool, 108 yd/99 m / 50 g), Color 1099, 100 g

Beads:
Approx. 80 beads, 6 mm. The beads shown here are from a long necklace purchased at H&M

NEEDLES
U.S. size 6 / 4 mm: set of 5 dpn

CROCHET HOOK
U.S. size G-6 / 4 mm

GAUGE
22 sts in stockinette = 4 in / 10 cm.
Adjust needle size to obtain correct gauge if necessary.

INSTRUCTIONS

Both wrist warmers are made the same way. Read through the instructions all the way to the end before you start to knit.

CO 44 sts and divide sts onto dpn. Join, being careful not to twist cast-on row; pm for beginning of rnd. Work 22 rnds in k1tbl, p1 ribbing. Next, knit 12 rnds. This stockinette section will be covered by the ruffles. Try on the wrist warmer and make sure that the bound-off edge fits around the lowest part of the hand without "billowing out" or drawing in. Instead of cutting the yarn and drawing it through the last st, place last st on crochet hook and ch 5. Now you can crochet the ruffles.

Ruffle

The ruffle is worked in treble crochet (British double treble). Do not crochet along the outer edge; instead, insert the hook into the stockinette knitted section—that is, go down into the stockinette base for every treble you crochet. The ruffle consists of one continuous line of treble, closely spaced together without any chain sts in between. The treble st line swings this way and that over the entire stockinette section as shown on the drawing. The ruffle winds all around the wrist warmer and ends where it started. Make a sample! That way, you'll see how easy it is to crochet a ruffle, how closely the trebles should be placed, and how closely to space the swinging lines. You can also use a sewing thread to baste the swing lines which you can then follow when crocheting the treble sts. Use dental floss or a wire needle to add a bead (see page 6) at the top of a treble on the st just worked. Place the beads as you like. On the model shown, there are are 4-8 trebles between each bead.

When the swinging line of trebles is back at the starting point, ch 5 and go down into the base again. Draw the yarn through to the WS. Cut yarn about 8 in / 20 cm from knitted surface and draw end through last st. Weave in all ends neatly on WS.

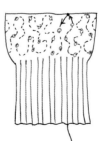

The ruffle consists of one long, swinging row of treble crochet. The row starts and stops where you bound off the last st of the stockinette section.

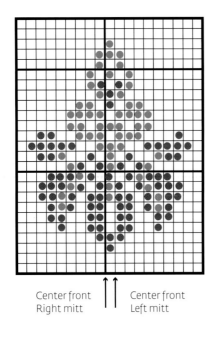

Center front
Right mitt

Center front
Left mitt

● Light purple bead

◉ Dark gray bead

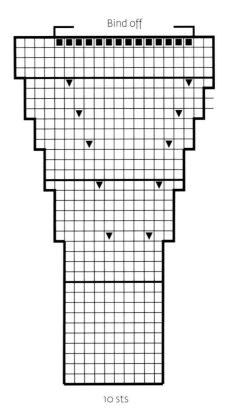

Bind off

10 sts

▼ Increase 1 st with M1

■ BO 1 st. After the bind-off, 6 sts rem

INSTRUCTIONS

Read through the instructions all the way to the end before you start to knit—several actions occur simultaneously.

With MC and the long circular, CO 40 sts. Work 6 rows back and forth in stockinette; the 1st row = WS.

On the 7th row (WS of the stockinette and right side of the mitt), change to CC and knit. *At the same time*, twist the row as you work across: After every 5th st, twist the whole left side of the work 360 degrees around. Twist so that the left side turns towards you, under the knitted fabric, and ends on the other side before you continue knitting as if nothing had happened. You might want to try a sample first. Making the twisted cast-on (also called a Latvian twisted cast-on) is unbelievably easy!

Row 8 (WS): Purl.

Rows 9-12: Knit, working back and forth so you create 2 ridges.

Change back to MC and divide the sts onto 4 dpn, with 20 sts for the back of the hand and 20 sts for the palm = (10 sts per dpn). The beginning of the rnd is centered on the inside of the wrist. Join and begin working in the round. You begin adding

beads while also working the thumb gusset.

Thumb Gusset

Knit 14 rnds with MC and then begin increasing for the thumb gusset (see chart above which shows the 10 sts for the right hand gusset). Increase with M1 between the 2 sts on the left needle. The increases are worked mirror-image on the left mitt. After completing thumb gusset, bind off the sts for the thumbhole so a total of 6 sts rem around the thumb opening. CO 4 new sts over the gap on the next rnd = 10 sts on each dpn. *At the same time*, when you've completed 19 rnds with MC, begin placing beads (see page 6) on the back of the hand as shown on the chart. Place bead and then knit the st. After all the beads have been placed, knit 7 rnds with MC. Change to CC and knit 1 rnd. Turn the knitting and knit back to the beginning of the rnd. Now knit back and forth 3 more times. BO on WS. BO knitwise.

Finishing

With CC, crochet a row of slip sts inside the edge around the thumbhole. Sew up any little holes around the thumbhole. Weave in all ends neatly on WS.

Cuffs with beads of many colors

Wrist warmers with a wavy edge and beads in a closely-worked design—almost like a hand garment for a folk costume. We know we'd never have managed to get these cuffs going if we'd had to thread all the beads in the correct order beforehand, even before casting on the first stitch!

DIFFICULTY LEVEL
Advanced

FINISHED MEASUREMENTS
Size S/M: approx. 4 in / 10.5 cm long with a circumference of approx. 6¼ in / 16 cm.
Size L: approx. 4 in / 10.5 cm long with a circumference of approx. 7½ in / 19 cm.
The model shown in the photos is size S/M.

MATERIALS
Yarn:
CYCA #1 (fingering) Sandnes Garn Sisu (80% wool, 20% polyamide, 191 yd/175 m / 50 g), Color 1088, 50 g

Beads:
Glass beads, 4 mm (Panduro):
Size S/M: 140 light purple, 195 dark gray, and 10 red beads
Size L: 168 light purple, 234 dark gray, and 12 red beads

NEEDLES
U.S. size 4 / 3.5 mm: long straight and set of 5 dpn

GAUGE
26 sts in stockinette with beads = 4 in / 10 cm.
Adjust needle size to obtain correct gauge if necessary.

INSTRUCTIONS

The numbers within parentheses refer to size L. Read through the instructions all the way to the end before you start to knit.

With long straight needles, CO 42 (52) sts. Always slip the first st of every row. The 1st row = WS and is purled. Work 6 rows total in stockinette.
On the 7th row (WS of the stockinette and right side of the cuff), knit and twist the row as you work across: twist the whole left side of the work 360 degrees around. Twist so that the left side turns towards you, under the knitted fabric, and ends on the other side before you continue knitting as if nothing had happened. You might want to try a sample first. Making the twisted cast-on (also called a Latvian twisted cast-on) is unbelievably easy!
Row 7: Sl 1 (edge st), *k5, twist*. Rep * to * until 6 sts rem, end k6.
Now divide the sts onto 4 dpn and join. Knit 1 rnd. BO the 2 edge sts (BO the 2 edge sts + 2 sts evenly spaced around) so that 40 (48) sts rem.
Purl 1 rnd.
Knit 2 rnds.
Continue knitting around, placing the beads (see page 6) as shown on the chart. Place bead and then knit the stitch. After the last bead rnd, knit 4 rnds, purl 1 rnd, knit 5 rnds.
BO knitwise. Weave in all ends neatly on WS. Sew the short ends of the twisted cast-on so twists match.

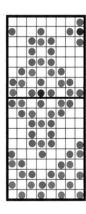

The repeat is worked 5 times total for Size S/M and 6 times for Size L.

◉ Light purple bead
◉ Dark gray bead
◉ Red bead

Fulled mittens, big and little

We think that everything that can be knitted can be knitted with beads! Fulled mittens are no exception from the rule. Here are women's mittens with an antler motif and children's mittens with pink beads.

DIFFICULTY LEVEL
Advanced

FINISHED MEASUREMENTS
Women's, Medium:
Size before fulling: approx. 6¼ x 16¾ in /
16 x 42.5 cm
Size after fulling: approx. 4½ in x 10¾ in /
11.5 x 27.5 cm

Children's, 4-6 years:
Size before fulling: approx. 5¼ x 10¾ in /
13 x 27.5 cm
Size after fulling: approx. 3¾ in x 8 in /
9.5 x 20.5 cm

MATERIALS
Yarn:
CYCA #2 (sport, baby) Sandnes Garn Tove (100% wool, 175 yd/160 m / 50 g)
Women's: 100 g Color 1035 (MC) and 50 g Color 1088 (CC)
Children's: 50 g Color 5229 (MC) and 50 g Color 5226 (CC)

Beads:
Glass beads, 4 mm:
Women's: 206 black and 38 white
Children's: 40-50

NEEDLES
U.S. size 6 / 4 mm: long straight and set of 5 dpn

TIP:
Heavy needles can easily slip out from the rest of the knitting while you form the bobbles— use light-weight wooden needles instead!

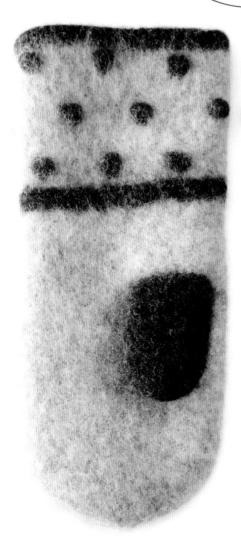

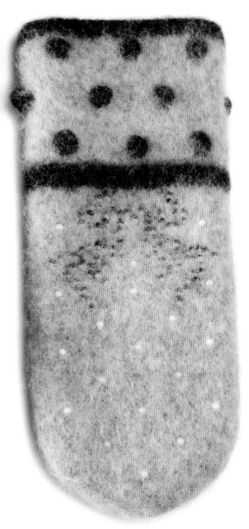

GAUGE

18 sts in stockinette = 4 in / 10 cm.
Adjust needle size to obtain correct gauge if necessary.

INSTRUCTIONS

Bobbles:
(K1, p1, k1) into same st.
Turn work and p3.
Turn work and k3.
Turn work and p3.
Turn work and sl 1, k2tog, psso.

WOMEN'S FULLED MITTENS

Read through the instructions all the way to the end before you start to knit.
With long straight needles and CC, CO 60 sts.
Knit 5 rows back and forth. Now divide the sts onto dpn with 15 sts on each needle = 30 sts for

109

the palm and 30 sts for the back of the hand. Join; pm for beginning of rnd. Change to MC and knit 5 rnds.

Make a rnd of bobbles on the 6th rnd: Begin with k5 in MC, (make 1 bobble with CC, k9 with MC) to last 5 sts; end with 1 bobble, k4. Since there are long floats between the bobbles, twist the yarns around each other at the midpoint between the bobbles.

Knit 12 rnds without bobbles.

Make bobbles on the next rnd: Make a bobble in the first st and then every 10th st so that the bobbles stagger over the first bobble rnd.

Knit 12 rnds without bobbles.

On the next rnd, make bobbles as for the first bobble rnd, beginning on the 6th and then every 10th st.

Knit 4 rnds without bobbles.

Change to CC. Knit 1 rnd. Purl 4 rnds but, *at the same time*, on the 1st purl rnd, decrease 3 sts with p2tog as follows: Decrease 1 st on the back of the hand and 2 sts on the palm = 29 sts rem for back of hand and 28 sts rem for palm.

Change to MC and knit 3 rnds without beads. Now place beads (see page 6) on the back of the hand following the chart. Place bead and then knit the st. The arrow at the side of the chart shows where to place a locking ring or thread marker for the 10-st thumbhole.

Right mitten: K2 at beginning of palm. With a smooth, contrast color waste yarn, k10. Slide the 10 sts back to left needle and knit with MC.

Left mitten: When 12 sts rem on palm, k10 with waste yarn. Slide the 10 sts back to left needle and knit with MC, k2 rem on palm.

Shape top of mittens following the chart.

When 9 sts rem, cut yarn, leaving an end 9¾ in / 25 cm long. Draw end through rem sts and tighten. Weave in the end neatly on WS. Using the cast-on end, seam the garter st band at beginning of mitten. Weave in all ends neatly on WS.

Thumb

Insert one dpn into row of sts below waste yarn and another dpn into sts above waste yarn. Carefully remove waste yarn. Divide sts onto 4 dpn; pick up and knit 1 extra st at each side = 22 sts total. With CC, knit 24 rnds. Work k2tog around. Knit 1 rnd and then finish as for the top of the mitten. Cut yarn; draw end through rem sts and tighten. Weave in all ends on WS.

Fulling

The mittens are fulled in the washing machine. Felting is often conflated with fulling. The process is the same for both—felting is the process for raw fibers and fulling is the name of the same process with woven, knitted, etc fabric.

Wool fulls best at 104°F/40°C when washed together with some stiff fabric—for example, jeans. Different machines and washing programs full differently, so it is impossible to give precise instructions. For the gray mittens, we recommend washing at 104°F/40°C, on a gentle cycle, without any pre-wash. Use regular washing powder and rinse (not Milo) with a stiff, old jeans vest. Don't forget that wet wool can be shaped! If you want to slightly change the length or width of the mittens, do this immediately after taking the mittens out of the washer, before you lay them out to dry on a heavy hand towel.

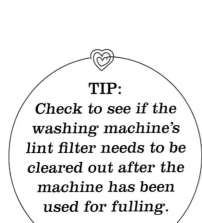

Black bead
White bead
K2tog tbl or ssk
K2tog

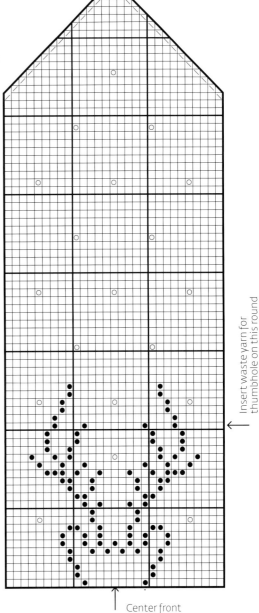

Insert waste yarn for thumbhole on this round ←

Center front

INSTRUCTIONS

CHILDREN'S FULLED MITTENS

For the smaller mittens, we chose purple and pink, colors that little ladies love! We purchased the glass beads in Lisbon. We love to visit sewing and yarn shops when we travel. The pink beads weren't very visible after the fulling but the mittens are quite fine nevertheless. No one will know what the beads looked like beforehand in any case.

Read through the instructions all the way to the end before you start to knit.
With long straight needles and CC, CO 48 sts. Knit 5 rows back and forth. Now divide the sts onto dpn with 12 sts on each needle = 24 sts for the palm and 24 sts for the back of the hand. Join; pm for beginning of rnd. Change to MC and knit 17 rnds.
Make a rnd of bobbles (see page 109) on the 18th rnd: Begin with k2 in MC, (make 1 bobble with CC, k5 with MC) around, ending with 1 bobble, k3.
Knit 4 rnds with MC without bobbles.
Change to CC. Knit 1 rnd. Purl 3 rnds.
Change to MC and continue around in stockinette. On the 5th rnd, begin placing beads (see page 6) randomly on the back of the hand. Place bead and then knit the st.
After 12 rnds with MC, make the thumbhole.
Right mitten: K2 at beginning of palm. With a smooth, contrast color waste yarn, k8. Slide the 8 sts back to left needle and knit with MC.
Left mitten: When 10 sts rem on palm, k8 with waste yarn. Slide the 8 sts back to left needle and knit with MC, k2 rem on palm.
After completing 32 rnds from the thumbhole, shape the top of the mitten. Work k2tog tbl at the beginning of the palm and back of hand and k2tog at the end of palm and back of hand = 4 sts

decreased per round. Decrease the same way on every rnd until 8 sts rem. Cut yarn, leaving an end 9¾ in / 25 cm long. Draw end through rem sts and tighten. Weave in the end neatly on WS. Using the cast-on end, seam the garter st band at beginning of mitten. Weave in all ends neatly on WS.

Thumb

Insert one dpn into row of sts below waste yarn and another dpn into sts above waste yarn. Carefully remove waste yarn. Divide sts onto 4 dpn; pick up and knit 1 extra st at each side = 18 sts total. With CC, knit 18 rnds. Work k2tog around. Knit 1 rnd and then finish as for the top of the mitten. Cut yarn; draw end through rem sts and tighten. Weave in all ends on WS.

Fulling

Full as for women's mittens.

Mittens with silver glass beads and lattice knitting

The cuffs are a little wider than the rest of the mittens on this pair—but they're such pretty cuffs that you won't want to hide them under coat sleeves!

DIFFICULTY LEVEL
Advanced

FINISHED MEASUREMENTS
When the mittens are laid flat, they are 10¾ in / 27 cm long. The cuff is 2½ in / 6.5 cm long and 4¾ in / 12 cm wide. The rest of the mitten is 4¼ in / 11 cm wide. This corresponds to Size M. You can adjust the sizing by working with larger or smaller needles.

MATERIALS
Yarn:
CYCA #3 (DK, light worsted) Sandnes Garn Smart (100% wool, 108 yd/99 m / 50 g), 100 g Color 1099 and 50 g Color 6162

Beads and Notions:
200 silver-dyed glass beads, 4 mm (Du Store Alpakka)
Gray or black sewing thread, sewing needle, and tapestry needle

NEEDLES
U.S. sizes 1.5 and 2.5 / 2.5 and 3 mm: long straight needles; U.S. 2.5 / 3 mm only: set of 5 dpn

GAUGE
24.5 sts in stockinette on larger needles = 4 in / 10 cm.
Adjust needle sizes to obtain correct gauge if necessary.

INSTRUCTIONS

The lattice-patterned cuffs are worked back and forth. After the mittens have been knitted, the cuffs are seamed at the center of the inside of the wrist where the rounds begin and end.

Lattice Pattern

The repeat is worked over 8 rows. The outermost st at each side is an edge st which is worked as k1tbl on the RS, where all the colors change. Sl 1 at at the beginning of all WS rows for an edge st. Make sure that the yarns for the lattice are loose enough that you can slip them without them drawing in. Make a swatch! All the slip sts in the lattice are slipped purlwise.

Row 1 (WS): Gray yarn. Edge st, p2, (sl 5 wyb, p1) across, ending with p1 and p1 edge st.
Row 2: Black yarn. Knit. Work the 1st rep without beads. For the 2nd and 3rd rep, place 1 bead (see page 6) on each gray st beginning with the 9th st (including edge st). Knit the st after placing bead.
Row 3: Black yarn. Purl.
Row 4: Gray yarn. Edge st, k1, sl 3 wyb, *lift the loose strand from the 1st row onto left needle and knit it tog tbl with the next st, sl 5 sts wyb*. Rep from * to *, ending with sl 3 wyb, k1, k1 (edge st).
Row 5: Gray yarn. P1, sl 3 wyb, *p1, sl 5 wyb*. Rep from * to * across, ending with sl 3 wyb, p1, p1 (edge st).
Row 6: Black yarn. Knit. Place 1 bead on gray sts (see page 6), beginning with the 6th gray st (including edge st). Knit the st after placing bead.
Row 7: Black yarn. Purl.
Row 8: Gray yarn. Edge st, k1, *lift the loose strand from the 5th row onto left needle and knit it tog tbl with the next st, sl 5 sts wyb*. Rep from * to *, ending with k1, k1 (edge st).
Rep Rows 1-8 3 times.

MITTENS

When you are knitting mittens, there are several steps you have to do at the same time.
Read through the instructions all the way to the end before you begin to knit.
With gray yarn and smaller size long needles, CO 65 sts. Purl 1 row and knit 4 rows. Change to larger needles and continue in lattice pattern. After completing the 3 rep of the 8-row pattern, continue with gray yarn. Purl 2 rows, and *at the same time*, on the 1st purl row, BO the 2 outermost sts at each side (the seam allowance). Divide sts onto 4 dpn. Join. Purl 2 rnds, decreasing 7 sts (with p2tog) evenly spaced around = 54 sts rem—27 sts for the back of the hand and 27 sts for the palm. Change to black yarn. Pm at each side. The rnd begins at the center of the palm. After working in stockinette with black yarn for 3¾ in / 8 cm, begin

the bead motif on the back of the hand, following the chart (place bead and then knit the st). At 3½ in / 9 cm, make the thumbhole.
Right mitten: K2 at beginning of palm. With a smooth, contrast color waste yarn, k8. Slide the 8 sts back to left needle and knit with MC.
Left mitten: When 10 sts rem on palm, k8 with waste yarn. Slide the 8 sts back to left needle and knit with MC, k2 rem on palm.
Sew the gray stitches (see chart) on the bead motif while the mitten is still open—about 6-7 rnds after the bead motif is complete.
Top shaping: the top of the mitten shaping measures 1½ in / 4 cm. Work until mitten is ½ in / 4 cm less than total desired length—usually when the mitten hits the top of the little finger. Shape the top at each side of both the back of the hand and the palm:
Decreasing at right side: K1, k2tog tbl (or ssk).
Decreasing at the left side: When 3 sts rem, k2tog, k1.
Decrease the same way on every rnd until 8 sts rem. Cut yarn, leaving an approx. 9¾ in / 25 cm end. Draw end through rem sts; tighten.

Thumb

Insert one dpn into row of sts below waste yarn and another dpn into sts above waste yarn. Carefully remove waste yarn. Divide the 16 sts onto 4 dpn; pick up and knit 1 extra st at each side = 20 sts total. Knit around until thumb is approx. 2½ in / 6 cm long or desired length. Shape as for top of mitten. Cut yarn; draw end through rem sts and tighten.

Finishing

Weave in all ends on WS.
Lay the short sides of the cuff against each other, RS facing RS so the beads and lattice patterns line up. Seam the cuffs by hand on the WS using sewing thread and back stitch. Open the seam and fold each seam allowance to the side and gently steam press.

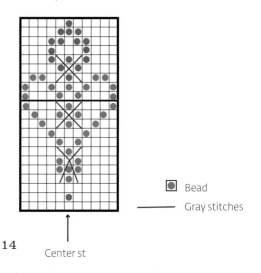

⊙ Bead
— Gray stitches

↑
Center st

The Selbu Rose pattern is also lovely without beads, but, with a few beads added, this well-known motif has an extra dimension that makes you take a second look. Both pairs of mittens are knitted with Sisu yarn with the same number of stitches, but one pair has a rolled edge and other has a doubled, picot, lower edge.

Mittens with Picot Edge: When the mittens are laid flat, they measure approx. 4 x 10¾ in / 10.5 x 27 cm, corresponding to Size S/M. The mittens shown in the photos have an edging slightly wider than the rest of the mitten. That's because the facing is worked in garter st.

MATERIALS
Mittens with Rolled Edging
Yarn:
CYCA #1 (fingering) Sandnes Garn Sisu (80% wool, 20% polyamide, 191 yd/175 m / 50 g), 50 g *each* of colors 1088 and 1002; approx. 10 g Color 4219

Beads:
40 red glass beads, 4 mm (Panduro)

NEEDLES
U.S. size 2.5 / 3 mm: set of 5 dpn

GAUGE
29 sts in stockinette on U.S. 2.5 / 3 mm needles = 4 in / 10 cm.
Adjust needle size to obtain correct gauge if necessary.

Mittens with Picot Edge
Yarn:
CYCA #1 (fingering) Sandnes Garn Sisu (80% wool, 20% polyamide, 191 yd/175 m / 50 g), 50 g each of colors 1042 and 1002; approx. 5 yd / 4.5 m Color 1099 (bead color)

Beads:
56 black glass beads, 4 mm (Panduro)

NEEDLES
U.S. size 2.5 / 3 mm: long straight needles and set of 5 dpn

GAUGE
29 sts in stockinette on U.S. 2.5 / 3 mm needles = 4 in / 10 cm.
Adjust needle size to obtain correct gauge if necessary.

If you want a slightly thicker pair of mittens, we recommend Smart yarn from Sandnes. With U.S. size 2.5 / 3 mm needles, the mittens will be dense and warm. With U.S. size 4 / 3.5 mm needles, the mittens will be slightly larger. No matter which needle size you choose, you'll need about 65 g of the dark main color—

Color 1088, for example—and about 60 g of the light color—for example, 1002—plus about 6 yd / 5.5 m yarn in the same color as the beads. Follow the instructions and charts for the gray/white Sisu mittens.

INSTRUCTIONS

MITTENS WITH ROLLED EDGINGS

The floats (yarn stranded between sts of different colors) are sometimes more than 7 sts in these mittens. To avoid rings and fingers catching in these long, loose strands inside the mitten, you should twist the yarns around each other when-ever there is a long float.

Read through the instructions all the way to the end before you begin to knit.

With black, CO 62 sts. Divide sts onto 4 dpn and join, being careful not to twist cast-on row. Knit 14 ends for the first rolled edge. Purl 4 rnds for the second rolled edge. Now work following the chart on page 121. See page 7 for an explanation of placing beads in the correct place when knitting with several colors of yarn Knit the st after placing the bead. See the instructions for the Mittens with Picot Edge for the thumb and shaping.

Finishing

Weave in all ends neatly on WS. Gently steam press the mittens except for the rolled edged.

MITTENS WITH PICOT EDGE

Read through the instructions all the way to the end before you begin to knit.

With gray and long straight needles, CO 62 sts

and knit 7 rows back and forth. Divide the sts onto dpn and join. Knit 2 rnds.

Make the foldline: (yo, sl 1, k1, psso) around. Count to make sure you still have 62 sts. (31 sts for the back of the hand and 31 sts for the palm). Continue, following the chart on page 120. See page 7 for an explanation of placing beads in the correct place when knitting with several colors of yarn. Knit the st after placing the bead.

Thumbhole: The thumbhole has 11 sts. Work the 11 marked sts as usual, but, on the next rnd, place the 11 sts on a holder. CO 11 sts in color sequence over the gap. Now there should be 31 sts for the palm. Continue in pattern following the chart.

Top Shaping: Work following the chart. When 6 sts rem (2 white and 4 dark), cut yarn leaving an end approx. 9¾ in / 25 cm long. Thread the white yarn into the tapestry needle and draw yarn to WS. Draw the dark yarn through rem sts and tighten. Slip yarn to WS through the hole at the top. Weave in ends neatly on WS.

Thumb: Work the 11 sts on the holder, pick up and knit 2 sts at the side, pick up and knit 11 sts across the top of the thumbhole + 2 sts at the side = 26 sts total. Divide the sts onto dpn with 13 sts for the front and 13 sts for back of thumb. Work following the thumb chart. Finish the top of the thumb as for top of the mitten.

Finishing

Sew the split at the lower edge. Fold the edge at the eyelet row and, by hand, sew down the facing on WS. Weave in all rem ends neatly on WS. Gently steam press mittens.

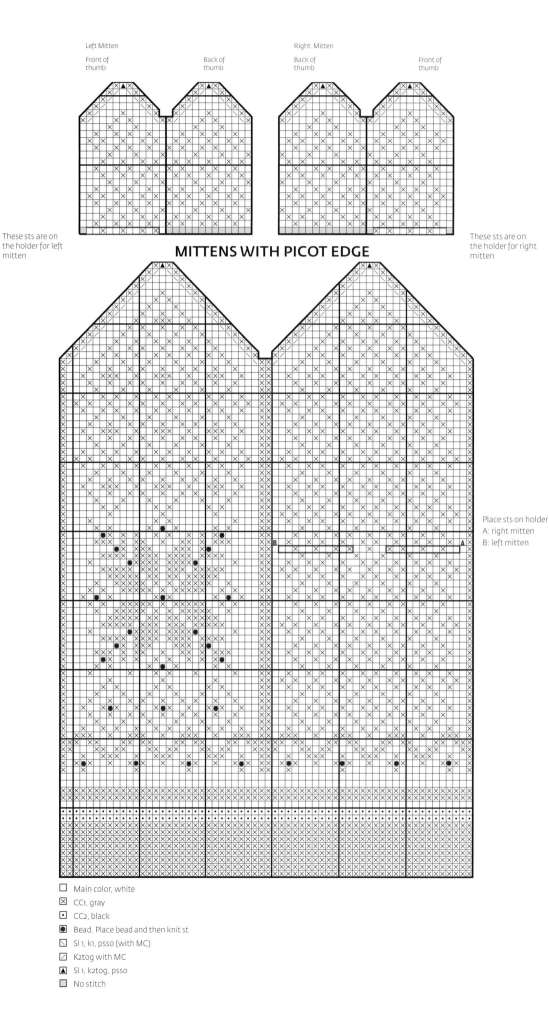

Left Mitten

Front of thumb

Back of thumb

Right Mitten

Back of thumb

Front of thumb

These sts are on the holder for left mitten

MITTENS WITH PICOT EDGE

These sts are on the holder for right mitten

Place sts on holder
A: right mitten
B: left mitten

☐ Main color, white
☒ CC1, gray
▪ CC2, black
◉ Bead. Place bead and then knit st
◲ Sl 1, k1, psso (with MC)
◱ K2tog with MC
▲ Sl 1, k2tog, psso
▨ No stitch

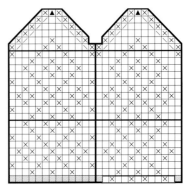

These sts are
on the holder

MITTENS WITH ROLLED EDGING

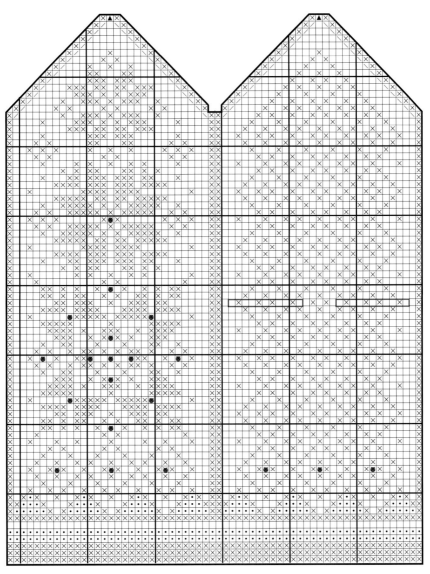

Place sts on
holder for thumb

☐ Main color, white

☒ CC1, black

⊡ CC2, red

◉ Bead. Place bead and then knit st

◱ Sl 1, k1, psso (with MC)

◲ K2tog with MC

▲ Sl 1, k2tog, psso

▧ No stitch

SOMETHING TO CARRY WITH YOU

For anyone who has something, here's what they need to carry it in!

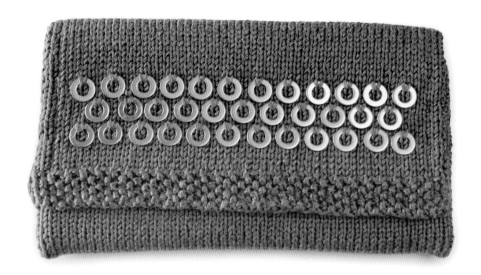

Heavy metal bags

Do you dig heavy metal? We can control our enthusiasm for the musicians, but, if we're talking about metal beads to add to our knitting, then we go all the way! We found our beads in a chain store and at the "Old Guy's Day Care" (otherwise known as Clas Ohlson, the Scandinavian hardware store).

DIFFICULTY LEVEL
Advanced

FINISHED MEASUREMENTS
Heavy Metal I: 11 x 6 in / 28 x 15 cm
Heavy Metal II: 9¾ x 6 in / 25 x 15 cm

MATERIALS
Yarn:
Heavy Metal I: Gray bag with metal rings
CYCA #3 (DK, light worsted) Garn Studio (Drops) Cotton Viscose (54% cotton, 46% viscose, 120 yd/110 m / 50 g), Color 19, 150 g.

Beads and Notions:
Metal rings M8 (Clas Ohlson), 15 mm, 2 packs
Table mat of stiff felt for lining, ⅛ in / 3 mm thick
(see Tips on page 125)

Zipper, 9¾ in / 25 cm long
Gray sewing thread, sewing needle

NEEDLES
U.S. size 6 / 4 mm: long circular or long straights

CROCHET HOOK
E-4 / 3.5 mm

GAUGE
20 sts in stockinette on U.S. size 6 / 4 mm needles = 4 in / 10 cm.
Adjust needle size to obtain correct gauge if necessary.

Heavy Metal II: Black bag with zipper
CYCA #1 (fingering) Sandnes Garn Sisu (80% wool, 20% polyamide, 191 yd/175 m / 50 g), Color 1099, 50 g
+

TIP
The table mat fabric
we used for lining
the bag is acrylic. It is
1/8 in / 3 mm thick.
We purchased it at an
interior furnishings
shop.

A patterned table mat works well as lining fabric for the bag. The zipper is sewn securely to the lining by hand.

CYCA #3 (DK, light worsted) Garn Studio (Drops) Cotton Viscose (54% cotton, 46% viscose, 120 yd/ 110 m / 50 g), Color 19, 50 g.

Beads and Notions:
Approx. 75 metal beads, 8 mm (see page 126)
Zipper, 9¾ in / 25 cm long
Black sewing thread, sewing needle
A small, zippered black evening bag to line knitted bag; chain link for handle; 2 key rings for attaching chain to bag

NEEDLES
U.S. size 10 / 6 mm: long circular or long straights

GAUGE
15 sts in stockinette on U.S. size 10 / 6 mm needles = 4 in / 10 cm.
Adjust needle size to obtain correct gauge if necessary.

INSTRUCTIONS

HEAVY METAL I
If you can knit with beads, you can, of course, knit with metal rings! Use them for a clutch bag. The other bag has a flat shopping bag as an inner bag but this bag is, instead, lined with stiff felt. The bag is knitted in one long piece with two strands of yarn held together and begins with a seed stitch edging. The rest of the bag is worked in stockinette: knit on the RS and purl on the WS. The knitting begins at the lower edge of the top flap.
With two strands of yarn held together, CO 57 sts (= 55 sts + 2 edge sts). Edge sts =Sl 1 st at the beginning of each row. Work 6 rows in seed st between the edge sts: (K1, p1) across; on subsequent rows, work knit over purl and purl over knit. Next, work 8 rows of stockinette.

On the 9th row of stockinette (RS), draw the 7th (including edge st) st through the first ring: hold the metal ring with the rounded side facing you, draw the stitch through the ring with the crochet hook, place st back on left needle and knit it. *K3, place ring on next st*. Rep from * to * across until 6 sts rem, end k6. Work 3 rows in stockinette. On the next row, place the metal rings centered between the rings on Row 9, with the first one placed on the 9th st (including edge st). Work 3 rows in stockinette.
Next Row: Work as for Row 9.
Continue in stockinette. When the piece measures 17¾ in / 45 cm, BO. Weave in all ends neatly on WS. Lightly steam press the bag on WS.

Finishing
The mat should be about ⅝ in / 1.5 cm smaller all around than the finished bag. Trim the lining along the long sides but wait to cut the short sides. Fold the knitted bag, with wrong side out, with 5¼ in / 13 cm long side seams. Using a doubled strand of sewing thread, sew the side seams by hand using back stitch and a ¼ in / .75 cm seam allowance. Turn the bag right side out and push the lining well down to the base (with WS facing WS) so that the knitted edge and the edges of the lining align along the opening of the bag for the zipper. You do not need to sew the lining at the sides, but, you should join the bag and lining, hand sewing with back stitches about ¼ in / .5 cm long, inside the outer edge at the zipper opening. Open the zipper and hand—sew it securely to the lining with back stitch, inserting the needle down at the same point where you just stitched. Check to make sure that the lining fits well into the bag before you sew down the other side of the zipper to the lining on the opposite side of the bag opening (see photo above).

The lining for the knitted bag helps the bag keep its shape so it won't be floppy. The bag we used as a lining had a sad plastic handle that we exchanged for a chain from another bag and attached with key rings.

The knitted fabric will naturally ruffle a bit around the edge of the lining along the sides of the flap. Join the lining and bag by hand sewing, with ¼ in / .5 cm long stitches inside the outer edge of the lining. In this case, you can use a single strand of sewing thread, basting by hand one way and then back. If you use sewing thread in the same color as the yarn, the stitches won't be visible on the RS. They will disappear between the stitches. Trim the lining along the short side so that it ends ¹⁄₁₆–⅛ in / 2-3 mm inside the edge with the bead knitting. Stitch by hand along this edge to finish.

HEAVY METAL II

With a simple bag from the nearest chain store as the starting point, you can knit your own exclusive version! The beads on our version (72 beads for knitting and 3 beads for the zipper pull) came from three simple bracelets (KappAhl).

The bag is worked back and forth in one wide piece, with doubled yarn, one strand from each ball. It is then joined, RS facing RS, along the base and then one side. The structure of the bead sec-

tion is the same as used for the gray collar shown on page 68.

Begin the bag at the lower edge. With one strand of each yarn held together, CO 77 sts or as many sts as you need to go around the lining bag. Knit 2 rows (seam allowance) and then continue in stockinette until the piece measures 2¾ in / 7 cm. Work 3 rows in reverse stockinette: knit on WS and purl on RS.

Now work in the structure pattern on page 68: Rows 1-4 and then Rows 1-2 so that you have 3 rows of beads. Work 3 rows in reverse stockinette and then continue in regular stockinette until the bag is long enough (on our model = 6 rows). BO on WS. Weave in all ends neatly on WS. Lightly steam press.

With RS facing RS, seam the bag on the base and along one side. Hand sew with back stitches and doubled sewing thread. Turn the bag right side out and insert the lining bag. Open the zipper and sew the two bags together by hand, along the zipper seam so that the lining bag is completely covered. Make a zipper pull with beads and left-over yarn.

Muff—nostalgia for frozen fingers

In very old photos of fine ladies in ankle-length winter coats, you can often see their hands covered by a muff. A muff will keep hands warm just as well these days! This one is lined with fur and has a zipper on the back so it also functions as a handbag, if you don't need it to protect against the winter chill.

DIFFICULTY LEVEL
Advanced

FINISHED MEASUREMENTS
The finished muff measures approx. 11 x 17¾ in / 28 x 45 cm when laid flat. The cord is about 55 in / 140 cm long.

MATERIALS
Yarn:
CYCA #3 (DK, light worsted) Sandnes Peer Gynt (100% wool, 98 yd/90 m / 50 g), Color 1099, 200 g
+
CYCA #3 (DK, light worsted) Sandnes Garn Alpakka (100% alpaca, 120 yd/110 m / 50 g), Color 6071, 50 g

Beads and Notions:
160 beads, 6 mm
Fur lining
Black sewing thread and sewing needle
Black zipper, 6 in / 15 cm long
Black Cotton fabric, 8 x 11¾ in / 20 x 30 cm

NEEDLES
U.S. size 6 / 4 mm: circular + 2 short dpn U.S. size 10 / 6 mm

CROCHET HOOK
U.S. size G-6 / 4 mm

GAUGE
18 sts in stockinette st on U.S. size 6 / 4 mm needles = approx. 4 in / 10 cm.
Adjust needle size to obtain correct gauge if necessary.

BEAD TIPS
The beads on this
model came from a
long H&M necklace.
We bought the
sheepskin lining
at IKEA.

The chart shows a repeating pattern. To the right side, vertical text reads:

1 repeat work 5 times total

Only the RS rows are shown on the chart. Begin each WS row with sl 1 as an edge st and then purl to end of row.

- ⊞ Edge st: sl 1 at beginning of every row
- ☐ Knit
- ☒ Purl

INSTRUCTIONS

Read through the instructions all the way to the end before you begin knitting.

With Black Peer Gynt yarn and U.S. 6 / 4 mm needles, CO 47 sts. Knit 6 rows back and forth. Now work following the chart.

NOTE: Only the RS rows are shown on the chart. WS side rows are worked as: sl 1 (edge st) and then purl to end of row. After completing 5 repeats of charted pattern, knit 2 rows. BO. Weave in all ends neatly on WS. Lightly steam press muff on WS.

Align the bound-off edge with the cast-on edge, right sides facing up. Seam the muff by hand, edge to edge from the outer side and then in to the opening (6¼-6¾ in / 16-17 cm long) for the zipper. Sew the pocket as shown in the sketch, machine-stitching if possible. Fold the lining down into the opening, pushing the knitted fabric a bit away from the center of the zipper. Open the zipper and hand sew it to the pocket securely, along both sides of the zipper opening.

The ruffle is crocheted as described on page 101. In this case, the ruffle is made higher by working a row of single crochet on top of the treble stitches. Begin crocheting ¼ in / .5 cm inside the outer edge. The outermost edge of the knitted fabric is without any ruffling because it is the seam allowance that will be folded over the lining edge later. Let the ruffle swing ¾-1¼ in / 2-3 cm in over the muff. First crochet the entire ruffle with treble crochet using Peer Gynt yarn without beads. Change to Alpakka and work 1 sc in each treble. Place the beads (see page 6) as you like. On our model, there are 4-8 sc between each bead.

Fur Lining

The lining is ⅜ in / 1 cm narrower but the same length as the knitted muff. Make a paper template that fits into your muff and stretch the template out on the back of the skin. Carefully cut the fur with a sharp hobby knife so the fur hair isn't damaged. Remove the paper template. With doubled sewing thread (or Goliath thread), hand-sew the lining, with edge to edge on the short sides so that you have a cylinder that fits inside the muff. You can use a regular sewing needle, but it's better to use a needle for sewing leather if you have one. Place the fur lining inside the muff, with the seam down at the base. The base is approx. 6 in / 15 cm below the zipper opening. Fold the outer edge, ¼ in / .5 cm, of the muff around the edge of the lining and sew the outer section and the lining together by hand, all around the opening.

Cord

The cord is knitted on U.S. size 10 / 6 mm double-pointed needles with two strands of Peer Gynt held together. CO 4 sts but do not turn. *Slide the sts back to front of left needle, pull the yarn behind the knitting, from the last st to the first, and k4*. No sts are slipped. Rep from * to * until the cord is approx. 55 in / 140 cm long or desired length. Insert the cord through the muff and tie the ends together or sew the ends together if you think the knot takes up too much room inside the muff.

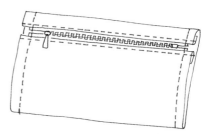

1. Work running stitch all around the fabric.
2. Fold in approx. ⅝ in / 1.5 cm seam on the short sides and then sew the zipper in securely as shown by the dotted red lines.
3. Fold the pocket so that the side seams are approx. 5½ in / 14 cm long. Seam the pockets together at the sides, with WS facing WS, as shown in the drawing.

TIP
You can use
the leftover
sheepskin as
a seat pad!

Single-crochet makeup bags

One pattern—three variations.
Who hasn't searched feverishly in their bag trying to find, for example, your lipstick? Crochet a makeup bag or two to contain all the small things in your purse so you know just where to find them. These crocheted makeup bags are small, soft, and take up almost no room.

DIFFICULTY LEVEL
Advanced

FINISHED MEASUREMENTS
Black makeup bag with tube beads: 6 x 5¼ in / 15 x 13 cm
Black makeup bag with turquoise beads: 7½ x 5½ in / 19 x 14 cm
Denim makeup bag with gray beads: 7 x 5½ in / 18 x 14 cm

MATERIALS
Black makeup bag with tube beads:
Yarn:
CYCA #1 (fingering), Sandnes Garn Mandarin Petit Cotton (100% cotton, 195 yd/178m / 50 g), Color 1099, 50 g

Beads and Notions:
63 yellow-green tube beads (Nabbi), size 5 x 5 mm
Zipper 6 in / 15 cm long
Sewing needle and sewing thread

CROCHET HOOK
U.S. sizes 7 steel-A and E-4 / 1.5-2 and 3.5 mm

Black makeup bag with turquoise beads:
Yarn:
CYCA #1 (fingering), Sandnes Garn Mandarin Petit Cotton (100% cotton, 195 yd/178m / 50 g), Color 1099, 50 g

Beads and Notions:
50 turquoise Kongomix beads, approx. 10 mm (Creativ Company)
Zipper 7 in / 18 cm long
Sewing needle and sewing thread

CROCHET HOOK
U.S. sizes 7 steel-A and E-4 / 1.5-2 and 3.5 mm

Denim makeup bag with gray beads:
Yarn:
CYCA #4 (worsted, afghan, Aran) Sandnes Garn Line (53% cotton, 33% other, 14% linen, 120 yd/110 m / 50 g), Color 6050, 50 g

Beads and Notions:
64-66 gray luxury wax beads, approx. 6 mm (Creativ Company)
Zipper 6 in / 15 cm long
Sewing needle and sewing thread

CROCHET HOOK
U.S. sizes 7 steel-A and E-4 / 1.5-2 and 3.5 mm

GAUGE
Black makeup bag with tube beads: 19 sts sc with U.S. E-4 / 3.5 mm hook = 4 in / 10 cm.
Black makeup bag with turquoise beads: 14 sts sc with doubled yarn and U.S. E-4 / 3.5 mm hook = 4 in / 10 cm.
Denim makeup bag with gray beads: 15 sts sc with U.S. E-4 / 3.5 mm hook = 4 in / 10 cm.
Adjust hook sizes to obtain correct gauge if necessary.

INSTRUCTIONS
See below for bead placement.

BLACK MAKEUP BAG WITH TUBE BEADS
The makeup bag is worked in the round.
With larger hook, ch 54 and join into a ring with 1 sl st. Begin each rnd with ch 1 (= 1st sc) and end with 1 sl st into last sc.
Rnds 1-2: Work round in sc without beads.
Rnd 3: Crochet in the beads as follows: Work 6 sc. After completing 6th sc, place 1 bead on the fine crochet hook and bring the sc through the bead.

Work 6 sc, place bead on the 6th sc as before. Continue as est around.
Rnds 4-5: Work around in sc without beads.
NOTE: On the 1st rnd following a bead rnd, make sure you always insert the hook down into the st with a bead on the same side of the bead—either in front of or in back of the bead.
Rnd 6: Work as follows: Begin with 3 sc, place bead on the 3rd sc. Work 6 sc and place 1 bead on the 6th sc. Continue as est around.
Rep Rnds 1-6 until the bag is desired length (our model has 7 rnds with beads).

Finishing
Finish with 1 rnd sl st. Cut yarn, leaving an 8 in / 20 cm end and draw end through last st to fasten off. Join the bottom of the bag with sl sts across. Weave in all ends neatly on WS. Sew in the zipper by hand, approx. 1¼ in / 3 cm from the top edge.

BLACK MAKEUP BAG WITH TURQUOISE BEADS
The Kongo beads have large enough holes that you can place the beads with a fine crochet hook. Because this bag is crocheted with two strands of yarn held together, it will be easier if you make two balls of yarn, each with two strands of yarn. The makeup bag is worked in the round.
With two strands of yarn held together, ch 54 sts. Join into a ring with 1 sl st. Begin and end the rnds as for the black makeup bag with tube beads. Work 6 rnds of sc. Pm at each side. Now begin adding the beads at the sides.
Insert the hook down into the sc that is directly over the marker and catch the yarn. You should now have 2 loops on the hook. Place a bead on the hook from the back, yarn over hook and through both loops and the bead. This is the same as a regular crochet, you just bring the yarn through the bead after the 2 strands.
Work in sc to the next marker and place a bead the same way. Complete the rnd in sc. Work 1 rnd sc without beads.
Work 1 rnd sc with 1 bead at each side. Work a rnd of sc without beads.
Add a bead on one side, 8 sc, place a bead on every other sc a total of 6 times (= 6 beads) centered on the front. Work 8 sc. Place 1 bead on the other side. Complete rnd in sc.
Work 1 rnd sc without beads. Continue as est, with a bead at each side and beads on the center front on every other rnd until there are 5 rows of beads (30 beads total) on the front (center front) of the makeup bag. Work 6 rnds sc with beads only at the sides on every other rnd (3 beads on each side).

Finishing

Cut yarn, leaving an end 8 in / 20 cm long. Draw end through last st and fasten off. Seam the bottom of the bag with sl sts. Sew in the zipper by hand approx. 1¼-1½ in / 3.5-4 cm from the top edge. Weave in all ends neatly on WS.

DENIM MAKEUP BAG WITH GRAY BEADS

Ch 54 sts and join into a ring with 1 sl st. Begin and end the rnds as for the black makeup bag with tube beads. Work 7 rnds in sc. Pm at each side.

1st Bead Rnd:

Work 2 sc, place 1 bead on the 2nd sc after working the st (when you have only 1 loop on the hook). Work 2 sc, place 1 bead on the 2nd sc. Continue as est until you've added 13 beads total and then work in sc to end of rnd.

Work 1 rnd in sc without beads.

NOTE: On the 1st rnd following a bead rnd, make sure you always insert the hook down into the st with bead on the same side of the bead—either in front of or in back of the bead.

2nd Bead Rnd: Work as for the 1st bead rnd. Work 2 rnds in sc without beads.

3rd Bead Rnd: Place beads as before. There are now 3 rnds of beads.

Work 14 rnd in sc (or to desired length) without beads. On the last rnd, place beads as for previous bead rnds but add beads on every st around.

Finishing

Cut yarn, leaving an 8 in / 20 cm end. Draw end through last st and fasten off. Seam the bottom of the bag with sl sts. Sew in the zipper by hand approx. 1½ in / 4 cm from the top edge. Weave in all ends neatly on WS.

135

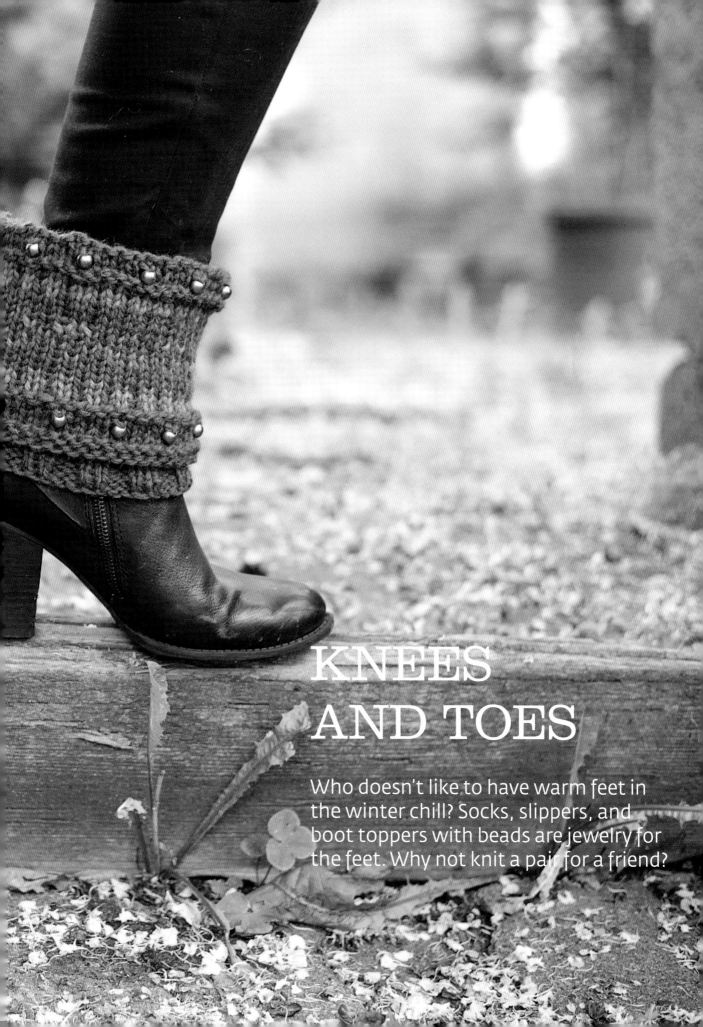

KNEES
AND TOES

Who doesn't like to have warm feet in the winter chill? Socks, slippers, and boot toppers with beads are jewelry for the feet. Why not knit a pair for a friend?

Tube socks/spiral socks

Totally simple, with no heel shaping. A sock to fit almost anyone.

DIFFICULTY LEVEL
Intermediate

FINISHED MEASUREMENTS
The socks are a total of 16½ in / 42 cm long. They will fit U.S. shoe sizes 5½-9 / Euro 36-40

MATERIALS
Mittens with Rolled Edging
Yarn:
CYCA #1 (fingering) Sandnes Garn Sisu (80% wool, 20% polyamide, 191 yd/175 m / 50 g), Color 6526, 100 g

Beads:
96 light turquoise metallic rocaille beads, 5 mm (Creativ Company)

NEEDLES
U.S. size 2.5 / 3 mm: set of 5 dpn

GAUGE
25 sts in ribbing on U.S. 2.5 / 3 mm needles = 4 in / 10 cm.

Adjust needle size to obtain correct gauge if necessary.

INSTRUCTIONS
For bead placement, see page 6. The socks are knitted in the round on 4 dpn. The spirals are formed by working 3 rnds in k2, p2 ribbing and then, on Rnd 4, shifting 1 st to the left.

CO 64 sts. Divide sts onto dpn and join, being careful not to twist cast-on row.
Knit 1 rnd. Work 1 rnd in k2, p2 ribbing. Now work following the chart on page 139. After working all the charted bead rnds, continue in ribbing without beads. When sock measures approx. 14¼ in / 36 cm, change to stockinette and shape toe as follows:

Decrease Rnd 1: (K6, k2tog) around = 56 sts rem.
Knit 3 rnds without decreasing.
Decrease Rnd 2: (K5, k2tog) around = 48 sts rem.
Knit 3 rnds without decreasing.
Decrease Rnd 3: (K4, k2tog) around = 40 sts rem.
Knit 3 rnds without decreasing.
Decrease Rnd 4: (K3, k2tog) around = 32 sts rem.
Knit 3 rnds without decreasing.
Decrease Rnd 5: (K2, k2tog) around = 24 sts rem.
Knit 2 rnds without decreasing.
Decrease Rnd 6: (K1, k2tog) around = 16 sts rem.
Knit 1 rnd without decreasing.
Last Decrease Rnd: K2tog around = 8 sts rem.
Cut yarn, leaving an 8 in / 20 cm end. Draw end
through rem 8 sts and tighten. Weave in all ends
neatly on WS.
Make another sock the same way.

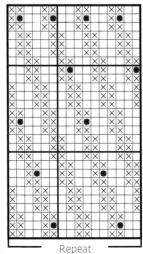

☐ Knit

☒ Purl

◉ Purl with bead

Repeat

Thick, soft, pretty, and warm slippers

These slippers sport Nabbi tube beads around the ankles. Tube beads from the toy shop can be used both for crochet and knitting. Perhaps you have some lying around? The slippers are fulled to make them extra thick and warm.

DIFFICULTY LEVEL
Intermediate

FINISHED MEASUREMENTS
These slippers will fit U.S. shoe sizes 6½-7½ / Euro 37-38 (see Tips on page 141).
Before fulling the slipper is 14¼ in / 36 cm long and 4¾ in / 12 cm high at the back.
After fulling, it measures 10¼ in / 26 cm and 3½ in / 9 cm

MATERIALS
Yarn:
CYCA #5 (bulky) Sandnes Garn Fritidsgarn (100% wool, 77 yd/70 m / 50 g), MC: Color 4300, 100 g and CC: Color 5229, 50 g

Beads:
26-30 tube beads (Nabbi)

NEEDLES
U.S. size 10 / 6 mm: circular and set of 5 dpn

CROCHET HOOK
U.S. sizes steel 7-A and 9-10 / 1.5-2 mm and 5.5-6 mm

GAUGE
14 sts in stockinette on U.S. 10 / 6 mm needles = 4 in / 10 cm.
Adjust needle size to obtain correct gauge if necessary.

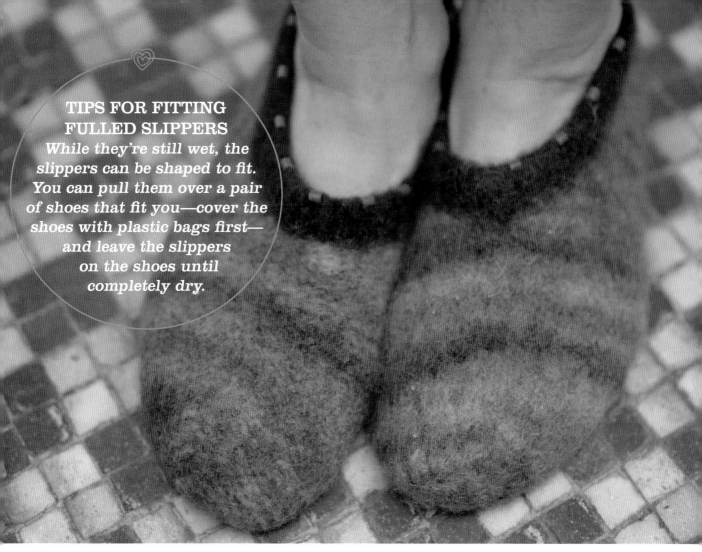

These slippers look just as good with either the right or wrong side out.

INSTRUCTIONS

Read through the instructions all the way to the end before you begin knitting. The slippers are worked both back and forth and in the round. With U.S. 10 / 6 mm circular and MC, CO 30 sts. Work back and forth in stockinette (knit 1 row, purl 1 row) until piece is approx. 7 in / 18 cm long. Now increase 1 st at the beginning and end of each RS row by working M1 between the 1st and 2nd sts and M1 before the last st. Increase the same way a total of 3 times = 36 sts. Purl 1 row after the last increase row. Knit 1 row and CO 4 sts at the end of the row = 40 sts. Divide sts onto 4 dpn and knit in the round for rest of slipper. Continue knitting around until entire piece measures 13-13½ in / 33-34 cm.

Toe Shaping:

Decrease Rnd 1: (K4, k2tog) around, end k4 = 34 sts rem.
Knit 2 rnds without decreasing.
Decrease Rnd 2: (K3, k2tog) around, end k2 = 28 sts rem.
Knit 2 rnds without decreasing.

Decrease Rnd 3: (K2, k2tog) around = 21 sts rem.
Knit 2 rnds without decreasing.
Decrease Rnd 4: (K1, k2tog) around = 14 sts rem.
Knit 1 rnd without decreasing.
Decrease Rnd 5: K2tog around = 7 sts rem.

Finishing

Cut yarn, leaving an end 9¾ in / 25 cm long. Draw end through rem sts and tighten.
Seam the slipper at center back. Weave in all ends neatly on WS.
Work 3 rnds of sc around the ankle with CC:
Work 2 rnds of sc around = approx. 39-40 sts around.
On the 3rd rnd of sc, place a bead on every 3rd st as follows: After a sc on 3rd st, place 1 bead on the thinnest part of the crochet hook and draw the st through the bead. Work 3 more sc and place bead on 3rd st as before. Continue as est around. Cut yarn and fasten off.
Make a second slipper the same way. Now it's time to full the slippers in the washing machine. For how to full, see page 110.

Boot toppers with beaded lace

Many tall boots have a thin lining in the leg and aren't particularly warm. You can avoid this by knitting a pair of boot toppers with a lovely alpaca yarn! These toppers have quite a long leg, but, of course, you can make them any length that suits your needs.

DIFFICULTY LEVEL
Intermediate

FINISHED MEASUREMENTS
The total length of these toppers is approx. 12¾ in / 32 cm. The bead panel (which is folded down) measures approx. 2½ in / 6 cm and the ribbing for the leg approx. 10¼ in / 26 cm.

MATERIALS
Yarn:
CYCA #3 (DK, light worsted) Sandnes Garn Alpakka Strømpegarn (sock yarn), (70% alpaca, 30% polyamide, 120 yd/100 m / 50 g), 50 g Color 1053 and 20 g Color 1042

Beads:
56 black beads, approx. 6 mm (these were taken from a bracelet)

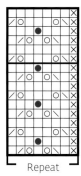

Repeat

All rounds shown on the chart

☐   Knit
☒   Purl
◎   Yarnover
●   Bead. Place bead and then knit st.
◣   K2tog tbl (or ssk)
◤   K2tog

NEEDLES
U.S. size 4 / 3.5 mm: set of 5 dpn

GAUGE
22 sts in ribbing on U.S. 4 / 3.5 mm needles =
4 in / 10 cm.

Adjust needle size to obtain correct gauge if
necessary.

INSTRUCTIONS
The cuff is knitted around on 4 dpn. For bead
placement, see page 6. Make both cuffs alike.

With Color 1042, CO 56 sts. Divide sts onto dpn.
Join, being careful not to twist cast-on row.
Knit 1 rnd, purl 2 rnds. Now work following the
chart. After completing charted rows, purl 1
rnd. Change to Color 1053 and knit 1 rnd. On the
next rnd, decrease 1 st at the beginning and 1 st
at the end of every rnd until 48 sts rem.
Now work in k1, p1 ribbing until the leg measures approx. 10¼ in / 26 cm or desired length.
BO loosely in ribbing. Cut yarn, leaving an end 8
in / 20 cm long. Weave in all ends neatly on WS.

Boot toppers

Sporty and warming boot toppers for wide boots.

DIFFICULTY LEVEL
Intermediate

FINISHED MEASUREMENTS
These cuffs fit all sizes. The total length of the boot toppers is approx. 11¾ in / 30 cm.

MATERIALS
Yarn:
CYCA #5 (bulky) Sandnes Garn Fritidsgarn (100% wool, 77 yd/70 m / 50 g), 100 g Color 6364 and 50 g Color 6052

Beads:
48 gray Kongomix beads, approx. 10 mm (Creativ Company)

NEEDLES
U.S. size 9 / 5.5 mm: 16 in / 40 cm circular; U.S. size 7 / 4.5 mm: set of 5 dpn

CROCHET HOOK
U.S. size A-D-3 / 2-3 mm

GAUGE
15 sts in stockinette on U.S. 9 / 5.5 mm needles = 4 in / 10 cm.
Adjust needle size to obtain correct gauge if necessary.

INSTRUCTIONS
Bead placement: Use the crochet hook (see page 6) to place bead on stitch. Place bead and then slip st to right needle. On the next rnd, knit the st with the bead in the back loop.

With larger short circular and 6364, CO 48 sts. Knit 4 rows back and forth (= 2 ridges). Now join to work in the round, being careful not to twist sts. Knit 1 rnd and then work following the chart. After completing charted rows, change to smaller dpn and work around in k2, p2 ribbing for approx. 6¾ in / 17 cm.
BO loosely. Cut yarn, leaving an 8 in / 20 cm end; draw end through last st. Weave in all ends neatly on WS. Make the second topper the same way.

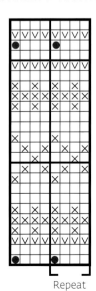

	6364 (knit)
●	6364 with bead (knit)
V	6364 purl
☒	6052 (knit)

Repeat

RESOURCES

Nordic Yarn Imports Ltd.
nordicyarnimports.com

Garn Studio (Drops)
garnstudio.com

Fire Mountain Gems and Beads
firemountaingems.com

Michaels
michaels.com

If you are unable to obtain any of the yarns or beads used in this book, they can be replaced with a yarn of a similar weight and composition, or beads of similar appearance. Please note, however, that the finished projects may vary slightly from those shown, depending on the materials used. Try yarnsub.com for yarn substitution suggestions!

For more information on selecting or substituting yarn, contact your local yarn shop or an online store; they are familiar with all types of yarns and would be happy to help you. Additionally, the online knitting community at Ravelry.com has forums where you can post questions about specific yarns. Yarns come and go so quickly these days and there are so many beautiful yarns available.

ACKNOWLEDGMENTS

A big thank you to everyone who has participated in and contributed to this book. To Sandnes Garn and Creativ Company who sponsored us by contributing yarn and beads. To the photo models, to May Linn Bang for technical editing, to Denise Samson for editing the charts.

And last, but absolutely not least, thank you to our photographer Guri Pfeifer for all the wonderful photos, and to Laila Sundet Gundersen for the stylish layout and interior design of the book. Thanks also to our beloved and hard-working editor, Kaja Marie Lereng Kvernbakken, who kept everything and everyone under control.